Winning Ways

Vol. 1: The Right Stuff

Innovative leaders discuss
Their Success Strategies

Michael B. Davie

Manor House Publishing Inc.

National Library of Canada
Cataloguing in Publication Data:

Davie, Michael B., 1954-
Winning Ways / Michael B. Davie.
Vol. 1: The Right Stuff.
Innovative Leaders discuss their Success Strategies

Includes bibliographical references.
Contents: v. 1. The Right Stuff.

ISBN 0-9731956-2-2 (v. 1)

1. Business people- - Canada--Biography.
I. Title. II. Title: The Right Stuff.

HC112.5.A2D39 2002   338.092'271   C2002-905153-3

Copyright 2002-10-15 by Michael B. Davie.
Published November 15, 2002
by Manor House Publishing Inc.
(905) 648-2193

First Edition. 224 pages. Approx. 40,000 words.
All rights reserved.
Book concept/cover design: Michael B. Davie.
Cover layout/realization: Richard Kosydar

Acknowledgements

This book would not have been possible without the full support and co-operation of the exemplary individuals featured in this book.

They neither paid nor received any payment for their co-operation, but chose to give freely of their valuable time and share their sound wisdom on ways to achieve success. My thanks to all of these leaders in their respective fields.

I'm also especially grateful to the many people, who decided to support this project by placing advance purchase orders for Winning Ways, sight unseen. Some participants placed no orders but gave valuable insight regarding achieving success.

The purchase orders we received in advance allowed us to govern our print runs efficiently and cost-effectively, ensuring enough books to meet demand but avoid a large inventory.

My thanks go to DeFeo Auto Service; Michael G. DeGroote; realtor Sue DePaulo, dentist Dr. Roland Estrabillo; the Hamilton Chamber of Commerce; Lakeport Brewing Corp.; Ken Lindsay and Mortgage Financial; mortgage broker Ray Puder ('Ray on Ray South') of Mortgage Financial; Rudy and Teresa Reimer; Rudy K. Reimer; and J. D. (Jim) Rundle, MBA, CGA, Certified General Accountant.

Thanks also to Richard Kosydar for layout assistance and technical expertise. As well, I appreciate the help extended by others, too numerous to name.

My thanks, as always, to my wife Philippa for her faith and encouragement in my many endeavours.
- **Michael B. Davie.**

Cover Photo Credits:

This book featured alternating cover photos. Cover/interior photo credits are as follows:

Sue DePaulo: Courtesy of Profiles of Success Magazine.
Lakeport/Teresa Cascioli: Courtesy, Lakeport Brewing.
Chamber of Commerce/JA (Downtown): Paul Sparrow.
Dr. Roland Estrabillo: Paul Sparrow.
Ken Lindsay/Mortgage Financial: Michael B. Davie.
Michael G. DeGroote: Philippa Davie.
Reimer family: Courtesy of Reimer Construction.

Winning Ways

Michael B. Davie

Manor House Publishing Inc.

By Michael B. Davie:

All titles published by Manor House Publishing Inc.,
unless indicated otherwise.

Non-fiction

Bushwhacked
Coping with the American Superpower
And other Post-Cold War Dilemmas

Winning Ways
Vol. 1: The Right Stuff

Following The Great Spirit
Exploring Native Indian Belief Systems

Political Losers
In Canada, U.S., Ukraine

Distant Voices
Canadian Politics On the Outside Looking In

Canada Decentralized
Can Our Nation Survive?

Quebec and Section 33
Why The Notwithstanding Clause Must Not Stand

Inside the Witches' Coven
Exploring Wiccan Rituals

Enterprise 2000
Hamilton, Halton, Niagara Embrace the Millennium

Success Stories BR
Business Achievement in Greater Hamilton

Hamilton: It's Happening* BR
Celebrating Hamilton's Sesquicentennial

Fiction

You're on my hit list for calling me
Creep
A Novel

The Late Man
A Novel

Archival

Print History
(Self-published, with more than 60 volumes and over 10,000 pieces of published writings)

BR = Published by BRaSH Publishing
* = With co-author Sherry Sleightholm
# = Written under the pen name I. Murderman

Manor House Publishing Inc.
(905) 648-2193.

Dedicated to
Michael G. DeGroote

Also dedicated to the late
D. O. Davis
Proud founder of
Junior Achievement
of Hamilton

About the author

One of Canada's most intriguing writers, Michael B. Davie is the author of such critically acclaimed business books as Enterprise 2000 and Success Stories.

The award-winning writer is also the author of such nationally important books as Canada Decentralized; and Quebec & Section 33: Why the Notwithstanding Clause Must Not Stand.

Other critically acclaimed books include: Distant Voices; Political Losers; Bushwhacked; Inside The Witches' Coven; Following The Great Spirit; and The Late Man, a novel.

Michael B. Davie is also a journalist with The Toronto Star, Canada's largest newspaper, reaching millions of readers daily.

The author has won dozens of awards for outstanding journalism. His work has also appeared in such major Canadian newspapers as the Halifax Chronicle-Herald, Montreal Gazette, Calgary Herald, Winnipeg Free Press, Edmonton Journal and Vancouver Sun.

Prior to The Star, he was an editor with The Globe and Mail, Canada's national newspaper with coast-to-coast readership.

Previous to The Globe, he spent 17 years with The Hamilton Spectator, where he won 28 journalism awards.

Prior to joining The Spectator, he spent five years with other publications, including the daily Welland Tribune where he was a reporter, columnist and editor.

He also served two years as regional news editor for one of Ontario's largest chains of community newspapers.

Born in Hamilton in 1954, Michael B. Davie's interest in writing began in early childhood. As a preschool child, he became withdrawn and was in a state of shock after his parents decided to divorce. During a visit to a community centre, the child opened the door to a room to find child psychologists had been studying him through two-way mirrors.

The young child then began closely observing other children and adults, studying their interaction and watching their stories unfold. By the late 1960s and into the 1970s, while in his teens, he was a contributing writer to counter culture publications.

He turned professional in the mid-1970s as Editor of The Phoenix serving Mohawk College of Applied Arts & Technology where he earned a Broadcast Journalism diploma.

He also holds a Niagara College Print Journalism diploma and degrees in Political Science from McMaster University where he was repeatedly named to the Deans' Honour List and won the Political Science Prize for outstanding academic achievement.

Michael B. Davie currently resides in Ancaster with his wife Philippa and their children Donovan, Sarah and Ryan.

Contents

Opening Notes

Chapter One
Junior Achievement
Learning to achieve success

Chapter Two
Rudy Reimer Sr.
Building a prosperous future

Chapter Three
Teresa Reimer
Success by design

Chapter Four
Rudy K. Reimer
Watching the rising son

Chapter Five
Sue DePaulo
Turning houses into homes

Chapter Six
Ken Lindsay
Home ownership help at Mortgage Financial

Chapter Seven
Dr. Roland Estrabillo
On the leading edge of dentistry

Chapter Eight
Lakeport Brewing
Pouring on the profits

Chapter Nine
Hamilton Chamber of Commerce
Helping businesses succeed

Chapter Ten
Michael G. DeGroote
Builder of empires

Manor House Publishing Inc.
(905) 648-2193.

Opening Notes

Ever wondered how some achieve success in life while others reach for the brass ring only to feel it slip from their grasp?

Winning Ways taps into the knowledge, expertise and advice of some very successful people.

In the following pages you'll encounter a wealth of information about earning wealth, about achieving last success, about making dreams come true and about conquering any obstacles in the way.

None of the participants telling their stories paid to go into this book. Nor did we pay them for their valuable advice and insight.

Instead, we selected some leading businesses, organizations, entrepreneurs and professionals – all leaders in their respective fields – to contribute to a discussion on the qualities that add up to success.

I set out writing this book in an effort to benefit Junior Achievement of Hamilton by creating a book filled with useful advice and tips youth can draw on for inspiration and education while setting on the road to success. This book also opens with a chapter on JA in hopes this worthy organization can make use of donated copies to promote its programs.

But somewhere along the way – the winning way – I found I too was learning a great deal about how to treat people and how to achieve success. This book is also of benefit to the population at large. It's a great chance to learn from those who have achieved lasting success in their respective fields of endeavour.

Simply put, this book is for all of us.

After reading in detail about the life stories, trials and tribulations encountered by our chapter participants, you'll find each chapter ends with a series of their tips for success. It's truly valuable reading that is sure to inspire and educate everyone.

The chosen participants in this book include Lakeport Brewing's lady president Teresa Cascioli; leading mortgage broker Ken Lindsay and Mortgage Financial; prominent dentist Dr. Roland Estrabillo; prominent real estate agent Sue DePaulo; Hamilton Chamber of Commerce; and leading commercial developer Rudy Reimer plus his entrepreneurial wife and son, who have each achieved their own enviable measures of success and have some interesting and insightful tips of their own to share.

And, we have billionaire businessman Michael G. DeGroote; who closes this book with a chapter detailing his life story, his setbacks, his business triumphs and his must-read tips for success.

Mike DeGroote was a particularly natural fit for this book: Not only has he achieved remarkable success; he's also been a major contributor to Junior Achievement of Hamilton over the past many years.

This book is dedicated to him and to the memory of the late D. O. Davis, who founded JA of Hamilton in 1968, and passed away earlier this year.

The successful people filling the chapters of this book know the importance of JA: Sharing one's insight with youth helps ensure the arrival of a new generation of knowledgeable entrepreneurs. Read on.

- **Michael B. Davie.**

Winning Ways

Chapter/Profiles
of Successful People

Tips on Achieving Success

A Learning Experience...
for Everyone

For
Junior Achievers

...everywhere!

Chapter One

Junior Achievement

Learning to achieve success

"All JA programs are unique and have a common theme – they reflect real life and are delivered by business volunteers – the front-line people who make the decisions."

Junior Achievement website: www.jahamilton.org

At a glance: Junior Achievement:

Junior Achievement of Hamilton:
Founded: JA Hamilton was started in 1968 by the late D. O. Davis, then a vice-president of Dofasco.

Claim to fame: Since the start of JA of Hamilton, more than 50,000 young people have participated in its various programs that bring business people and youth together to learn the ways of commerce.

Programs: The Company Program allows high school age students to temporarily establish their own small business and learn from the experience with the advice of local business people volunteers. Other programs assist in the formal education process and encourage pre-high school students to stay in school.

Mission: JA's mission is to inspire and educate young people to value free enterprise; understand business and economics; and develop entrepreneurial and business leadership skills.

For More information:
Contact: Junior Achievement of Hamilton:
Phone: (905) 528-5252.
Fax: (905) 528-7787.
Address: 2 King St. West, 3rd floor, Cinema building, Lloyd D. Jackson Square, Hamilton, Ont., L8P 1A1.
Website: www.jahamilton.org

Chapter One

Junior Achievement
Learning to achieve success

Not all business lessons are best learned in a classroom. Often the best advice comes directly from those who have been there, done that, and lived to tell about it.

That's core to the guiding philosophy behind Junior Achievement, a venerable non-profit organization that brings business leaders and youth together in a unique learning experience.

And these highly educational JA programs give their youthful participants the rare opportunity to truly experience what it's like founding and then running their own small business and grappling with everything the reality of such a worthy undertaking clearly implies.

In recent years, young people taking part in Junior Achievement of Hamilton programs have been able to learn from the expertise earned by such prominent area business leaders as Tim Hortons co-founder Ron Joyce, billionaire businessman Michael G. DeGroote, and many others who lend financial support, time and advice to JA programs.

And when Joyce, DeGroote or another business leader takes the stage at a JA event to relate their life story and explain how they overcame obstacles to achieve success, their message is of great value to the young JA participants.

Simply put, it fuels the participants' quest for knowledge of how businesses work and achieve success.

Focusing on high school students

Many Junior Achievement programs focus on high school age children age 13-19, during a pivotal time in their lives.

After all, it's during the high school years when they're encountering mounting scholastic workloads, peer pressures of all sorts, self-doubts, personal/physical changes and questions concerning what career they'd like to eventually pursue and what exactly they'd like to achieve in life.

These young people are at a cross-roads in life: No longer little children but not yet mature adults; grappling with uncertainties; exploring a range of options; and in need of positive direction.

And they find that positive direction is readily provided by Junior Achievement programs that give them with hands-on experience towards founding and running their own temporary small business venture.

For many of these young people, this is often their first exposure to the business world. Depending on their background and personal tastes, they may not have ever considered a business career as a meaningful option.

But through JA, they participate in running a business, get their commercial feet wet, gain an understanding of the world of commerce, and are better able to determine if they'd like to consider a career in business as one of their top employment choices.

Taking the mystery out of business

At the very least, JA programs give them some familiarity with a business world they may well have previously found mysterious and confusing, perhaps even bewildering.

The participants gain insight into the workings of business and an appreciation of what it takes to develop and market a product or service.

They also take part in problem-solving and marketing tasks outside of a classroom setting. They're in charge of the companies they start-up and that means thinking on their own, employing their own logic and creativity, tapping into their budding people skills and leadership traits.

Perhaps the best-known JA program is its flagship Company Program, in which 20 or more high school students get together one evening per week for 24 weeks to found, own and operate their very own company.

Beyond offering a degree of on-the-job experience, the Company Program – under the guidance of business expert volunteers – also builds teamwork skills, self-confidence and self-esteem as the company partners work together to choose and market a product; track expenditures and finances; pay bills and wages; and, ideally, go on to achieve the goal of earning a profit.

The participants also get the opportunity to make new friends, consider different points of view and take part in JA conferences and awards events.

In Hamilton, JA of Hamilton's Company Program runs each year from late October through to May. It operates out of three area centres: the JA of Hamilton headquarters at Lloyd D. Jackson Square; the North Hamilton Community Health Centre and the Stoney Creek Optimist Club House (for more detailed information, contact JA at: 905-528-5252).

Opening eyes to opportunities

For the participants, the Company Program opens their eyes to a world of business opportunities and an educational process that for some is a whole lot more interesting and fun than school.

And, speaking of school, another reason the JA program focuses on high school students is to instil a greater appreciation of formal education and help stem Hamilton dropout rates that are still hovering around 30 per cent of the student population.

JA also aims to improve the percentage of students opting for post-secondary education beyond the current 34 per cent participation rate. In contrast, an impressive 83 per cent of JA participants go on to post-secondary education or trade-related training.

While the value of education is certainly an important focus, so is the chance for youth to actually start up and run their own temporary firm.

Indeed, the Company Program presents a truly challenging and rewarding process: The youthful participants take well-earned pride in the companies they create. But now, how do they deal with the realities of marketing? How do they bring their product or service to the buying public? What is the market demand for their goods and services?

As well, how do they best exploit each of their partners' strengths – and how do they resolve any problems that arise?

Gaining a better understanding

For the first time in their young lives, they may gain a real and lasting understanding of the role of business in our economy, in our workplaces, in our nation, in our lives.

Yes, it's a learning experience. And it's a learning experience unlike any other because it can impart and develop business skills that will literally last a lifetime.

In essence, Junior Achievement allows youth to explore the world of business with the help of expert navigators in the form of business leaders to generously contribute their time and expertise.

Some of the very real benefits to youth are detailed on JA's website – www.jahamilton.org - that advises its young participants: "JA empowers you and gives you the tools you need to help make the decisions to shape your future.

Whether you have one career throughout your life or five, whether you end up working at the local coffee shop or owning it, the skills and attitudes you learn in Junior Achievement last a lifetime."

The website adds: "All JA programs are unique and have a common theme – they reflect real life and are delivered by business volunteers – the front-line people who make the decisions."

In addition to the after-school Company Program, Junior Achievement offers other programs, including the Student Venture program, which offers students the chance to start up a classroom-based business enterprise and develop the entrepreneurial skills needed to become a successful business owner and operator.

Stay in School

Yet another program is the Economics of Staying in School program aimed squarly at Grade 8 students.

The ESIS program focuses on keeping students in school by taking a logical rather than preachy stance: Students receive help in developing a positive attitude toward school and are given insight into the low-wage and high-living-costs scenario they can expect to face if they drop out and try living on their own.

As well, the ESIS program helps students understand the correlation between a good education and a good job. They get to contemplate what type of career might interest them – and what educational qualifications they would need to pursue this goal. Help is also offered in developing job interview and resume-writing skills.

Other JA programs focus firmly on improving students' learning capabilities, helping them cope with changes to the Ontario curriculum and other scholastic challenges.

In these programs, an outside consultant – a business person – is brought into the classroom to work with the teacher in a bridge capacity, relating work experiences that help illustrate concepts taught in the classroom.

JA provides training sessions for teachers and consultants, helping them plan the most effective ways to link learning with real-life experiences. But demand for this program often exceeds supply, so it's best to contact JA early and plan ahead.

Program popularity growing

In fact, all of the various programs offered by Junior Achievement of Hamilton have grown sharply in popularity.

For example, in the early 1990s, 1,500 young people participated in JA programs.

A mere 10 years later, that number had more than tripled to over 4,500 participants and has been estimated at 5,000 participants for 2002.

And there's no sign of this phenomenal growth rate slowing down.

Indeed, each and every year, a new group of young people emerges to take part in the various Junior Achievement programs.

In fact, Junior Achievement itself is by far the oldest and fastest-growing economic education program for young people in the entire world due, in part, to the contribution made by the many caring companies and business people who support this organization that does everything from help kids in school to assisting them with starting up and running their own small business.

JA a true bargain

Even while increasing its growth rate of active participants, JA of Hamilton has also endeavoured to hold the participation costs of its programs, in essence building tomorrow's business leaders at yesterday's prices.

While it can cost as much as $7,000 to put a student through the Hamilton education system, putting a student through JA can cost as little as $100 – a sound investment.

Special events

In addition to its programs, JA of Hamilton hosts several annual events, including the Annual Golf Classic and the Governors' Dinner, featuring inspiring keynote speakers. For example, the April of 2002 Governors' Dinner featured Herman Boone, head coach of the legendary Titans football team that combined three U.S. high schools – two white and one black – into the racially mixed T. C. Williams High School in Virginia. By putting aside prejudices and learning to work together, the team won the state championship – a truly inspiring tale.

Serving Hamilton and area since 1968, Junior Achievement of Hamilton is a charter member of the Junior Achievement of Canada national organization. Canada itself is a proud member nation of Junior Achievement International.

All JA programs emphasize the importance of a good education. The JA programs also help students develop positive attitudes and enthusiasm for the necessity of lifelong learning.

And all of the participants' temporary companies fulfill the JA mandate of providing their youthful business executives with the rewarding experience of operating a company; producing, marketing and selling products; and managing inventory, costs, revenue and consumer demand.

This true-to-life business experience has a way of bringing out hidden talents in student participants while helping them to believe in themselves.

A chance to taste success

"They're tasting success and it's giving them confidence," vice-principal Lorne Evans once said of a group of youthful JA Student Venture program participants from Mountain Secondary School.

Carol Montag, a former president and CEO of Junior Achievement of Hamilton, recalls the JA of Hamilton experience as offering "an effective way to build an awareness and appreciation of business – I love watching the students' enthusiasm and their self-confidence grow."

The evidence also suggests students love the JA experience as well: The current participation rate of more than 5,000 children a year marks a five-fold increase over 1,000 participants in 1987 when Montag had joined JA.

Founded in 1919 in Springfield, Mass., Junior Achievement began in Canada in 1955 and now boasts more than 700,000 participants across Canada every year. This independent, not-for-profit organization supported by business also attracts about 4-million children globally.

Indebted to D. O. Davis

In 1968, Junior Achievement of Hamilton was founded by D. O. Davis, then a vice-president at Dofasco, who built the not-for-profit organization from scratch into the multi-program entity it is today.

He would continue to play an extremely important and influential role in JA right up until his passing in the summer of 2002 in his 99th year.

Junior Achievement of Hamilton is indebted to D. O. Davis and to the many businessmen and women who selflessly lend their expertise and support to JA programs.

In Hamilton, the JA program has enjoyed working partnerships with McMaster University and Mohawk College.

Driven by volunteers

As well, about 60 local businesses provide volunteer consultants. Some of these supporters also have a presence on the JA Hamilton Board of Directors or the JA Board of Governors, including representatives from The Hamilton Spectator; Torstar; Dofasco Inc.;

Fluke Transport; Morgan Firestone Foundation, 900 CHML Radio, Orlick Industries, Embree Industries and the Bank of Montreal, to name but a few.

Montag says JA's success at reaching young people is the hands-on involvement of the youthful participants.

She says volunteers provide guidance and the student participants use this advice to create their own business ventures under the Company Program.

How the Company Program works

"We provide the material, curriculum public speaking tips and concepts and the volunteer business people teach them to the students who basically put all of it into action," she explains.

"The students come up with the idea for a company and they sell shares to finance their business," she adds.

"They manufacture, market and sell a product. Then, after 26 weeks they liquidate the company and the investors are paid back. It really is experiential learning. The best way to learn anything is to actually do it."

JA values more relevant than ever

Montag says the basic values driving JA are more relevant than ever before.

"More people will be self-employed in the new generation than in any generation preceding it," she notes, "and some experts say as many as one person in three will be self-employed."

"Young people, parents and teachers know that

experience is crucial to become workforce ready. At Junior Achievement, we teach entrepreneurship. Our students can increase the likelihood of being hired or successfully creating their own job."

Over the past decades, Junior Achievement of Hamilton has developed into a community of past and present participants and volunteers.

Alumni Association

The JA Hamilton Alumni Association was formed in 1999 to locate the more than 50,000 people who have participated in JA of Hamilton since this organization was founded in 1968.

Today, the alumni association has more than 350 active members from all walks of life and from around the world.

The JA alumni's mission is to promote Junior Achievement of Hamilton's mandate of providing hands-on economic education for youth by encouraging the involvement of past participants.

As well, the alumni association endeavours to reunite members with past friends and associates and to provide them with a meeting place for their mutual rediscovery.

Membership in the alumni association is open to all past members of JA of Hamilton, including, of course, graduate achievers, volunteers, professional staff and board members.

Volunteers essential to success

Volunteers are included for good reason: They are absolutely crucial to the ongoing success of JA of

Hamilton. Always have been. Always will be.

By donating their time and resources, their expert advice and willingness to help, these volunteer business people provide the essential guidance needed to steer participants' businesses on the road to success.

Some of the business volunteers also pay sponsorship fees to fund programs.

The cost of sponsorship really isn't all that expensive. Not when you consider a company can divert just a fraction of the funds it would normally devote to sending personnel to conferences to instead support JA.

Perhaps the biggest single difference between throwing money at a conference and sponsoring JA is that the money spent on JA is an investment in youth that is sure to have lasting value.

And the benefits aren't all one-sided: Simply by providing a staff member – or yourself – as a JA volunteer business expert, you're taking part in an exercise that will confer valuable leadership growth and organizational benefits to your own company.

Why do the volunteers donate so much of themselves?: They understand the importance of JA.

Simply put, an investment in JA today is an investment in the business leaders of tomorrow.

Rudy Reimer

Chapter Two

Rudy Reimer Sr.

"To get ahead in life, sometimes you have to do a little homework. My hobby was learning everything I possibly could about construction – and that's still my hobby. For me, business and serving the community is my greatest hobby - and my greatest challenge."

- **Rudy Reimer.**

At a Glance: Rudy Reimer Sr. and Reimer Construction:

Rudy Reimer
Age: 65
Title: President & CEO, Reimer Construction Limited.
Awards: Reimer is a proud recipient of the highly prestigious *Queen's Golden Jubilee Medal*, honouring his "significant contribution" to Canada and his fellow Canadians. Canada's Governor General has presented him with the ***Commemorative Medal For The 125th Anniverserary Of The Confederation Of Canada***, to recognize his "significant contribution to compatriots, community and to Canada." You can also find him listed in the influential *Who's Who National Registry* under executives and professionals of note. And he's been honoured with the coveted ***Lifetime Achievement Award*** from the Burlington Chamber of Commerce and he's won many other awards - far too many to list.
Claim to fame: Major developer of commercial and residential projects. Commercial project's tenants read like a Who's Who of Canadian business leaders. He's transformed Burlington's skyline and is turning the city into a major commercial centre.
Financial Data: Undisclosed. Successful Private firm.
Personal: Resides in Burlington with wife Teresa Reimer. Father of Rudy K. Reimer and Darlene Reimer.
For More information:
Contact: Reimer Construction: (905) 336-8775
Fax: (905) 336-7936.
Address: 9th Floor, Reimer Millennium Tower, 5500 North Service Road, Burlington, Ontario, L7L 6W6.

Chapter Two
Rudy Reimer Sr.
Building a Prosperous Future

Rudy Reimer escaped war-torn Germany, went from rags to riches in Burlington, and so transformed the local landscape it's been dubbed 'Reimer Country'.

Reimer is the dynamic developer of numerous office complexes lining the highway from Burlington to Oakville. And when it comes to doing business and serving the community, he's a gold medal performer.

In October 2002, Reimer, 65, was awarded the highly prestigious ***Queen's Golden Jubilee Medal*** in Royal recognition of his "significant contribution" to Canada and his fellow Canadians.

The same month, Canada's Governor General presented him with the ***Commemorative Medal For The 125th Anniverserary Of The Confederation Of Canada***, to recognize his "significant contribution to compatriots, community and to Canada."

And just a few months earlier he was named the first-ever recipient of a ***Lifetime Achievement Award*** from the Burlington Chamber of Commerce, honouring his "dedication, vision and passion as a developer."

In addition to his seemingly endless string of accolades, awards and medals, Reimer is listed in the highly influential ***Who's Who National Registry*** under prominent North American executives/professionals.

A generous contributor to many worthy causes, Reimer recently donated funds to erect a cross, on the QEW near Vineland, bearing the message 'Jesus loves you'. His donation came at the request of Pastor Henry Wiebe, formerly Reimer's Sunday school teacher.

"He taught me Christian values that have stayed with me my whole life - I'm glad to help," notes Reimer, patriarch of a family of business leaders including wife Teresa, head of T. Reimer Design Consultants Inc.; son Rudy, president of R. K. Reimer Developments; and son-in-law Randy Heine, president of Crystal Ridge Development Services.

As he surveys the stretching landscape from the glass walls of his penthouse office, Reimer exudes the self-confidence of a savvy dealmaker and developer who has achieved enviable business success.

But how he survived wartime persecution and poverty to rise to his position of power and influence is one of the most intriguing and inspiring stories you're ever likely to read.

Reimer's Challenging Life

Reimer's life story begins in southern Ukraine, in a small village near the Black Sea, where he was born to a Mennonite family that spoke a Low German dialect, somewhat similar to Dutch.

He was the family's only son although the Reimers also had two daughters: Frida, a former teacher, would later marry a produce cultivator in Beamsville, Ontario. Marianne would marry a heart specialist and general surgeon in Virginia, USA.

Since Ukraine was then part of the Russia-controlled Soviet Union, at school, Reimer had to learn Russian in order to comprehend classroom instruction.

The family lived a crowded existence in a house offering less than 700 square feet of living space – about the size of his current bathroom.

As a religious minority in Ukraine, the Reimer family was subjected to persecution. And it soon intensified.

In the early 1940s, with World War II raging, the Russians periodically walked into his relatives' homes and removed one family member or another for questioning. Jail terms often followed. Some relatives were never seen or heard from again.

"Then," Reimer recalls, "when I was about five, the Germans came marching into our German-speaking village in Ukraine. They told us: 'You're Germans – you're coming with us,' and we were evacuated out of Ukraine and taken to Germany."

The final 200 kilometres of their three-week-long journey was on foot across rough terrain.

Refugee camp

They would spend the next year living in barracks housing in a refugee camp in Germany.

At age 6, Reimer and family were again on the move just as World War II was grinding to a close and he recalls seeing "many rockets and bullets fly through the air – that was when we had to go to the underground shelter for security."

"I can remember walking past Dresden and through Berlin when these cities were being bombed," he recalls, nearly 60 years later in an interview at office in Burlington.

"What I remember most is how the cities lit up when they were bombed, and the glow as they burned," he adds.

Father taken prisoner

Although a peaceful Mennonite, his father, Peter Reimer, was forced to join the German army – the alternative to not enlisting was a bullet through the head – and he was sent to the Russian front in 1944, just one month before the war ended.

At that time, while his father served on the Russian front, Reimer and his mother and sisters moved into the home of an aunt, who was married to a German army officer.

Then, in the dying months of the war, the Russians captured Peter Reimer. And when they questioned him, he answered first in German, then in Russian. This proved to be a nearly fatal mistake.

It led his captors to accuse him of being a spy. A gun was pointed towards his head.

The trigger was pulled. And the bullet shot through his hat, missing his head entirely.

Having cheated death, Peter Reimer was allowed to live – but given a life sentence with hard labour as a Siberian Gulag prisoner.

"We didn't even know he'd been captured," Reimer recalls.

"We had no knowledge whatsoever of his whereabouts for 10 years – we could only assume he was alive, as my mother had the belief that God would bring them safely together again, alive and well."

By this point, Reimer was still a young child. He was left with his mother Anna and sisters Frida, 4, and Marianne, 1, in what would become the partitioned, Soviet-controlled East Berlin area.

Decided to escape

The war ended, but the Reimer family's troubles continued. Anna Reimer was questioned by the Russian occupiers and made her husband's mistake of answering them in Russian. She was taken away for questioning.

Anna Reimer was released temporarily after a prominent relative intervened. She was told to return to the police station the following morning.

"My mother knew where this was likely to end up," Reimer asserts, "so she decided we would all escape from the Russian sector near the Berlin area."

Anna Reimer and her three children walked in the dark to the train station where the family hid in the bushes.

As the train pulled into the station and slowed down, the mother and her three children crawled quickly between the slowly moving wheels of a boxcar, emerging on the other side where the boxcar doors were located.

"My mother knocked, the door opened and we were pulled inside," Reimer recollects.

Guard pointed a gun at them

"A moment later, the door was wrenched open and a guard pointed a gun right at us," Reimer adds, his face drawn tight from the vivid memory.

"The guard was very angry and said he didn't remember us getting on the train and then he demanded a full passenger count – we all had a very sick feeling," he recalls.

"But one of the men in our boxcar told him there would be no counting as everyone was legally on board," he adds.

"The guard then just shrugged his shoulders and walked away."

Once they were safely in what was then West Germany, Reimer excelled in school and skipped several grades during the years the family lived in that country.

Then, in 1949, the family immigrated to Canada – the trip was paid for by church groups as the family had virtually no money – and moved in with an uncle in a small Mennonite community at Camden, which is on the ouskirts of Vineland, Ontario.

The Promised Land

"The vision I had of Canada at that time was that all the telephone poles were made of gold," Reimer recalls. "That was the only disappointment that we have received in Canada."

Reimer took quickly to his adopted country, working hard to learn to speak English and eagerly walking six kilometres to school.

He also eagerly grasped the opportunities he saw around him, including a chance to get involved in some summer work as a farm labourer.

"During summer holidays, I had the great privilege of thinning peaches, picking strawberries and other fruits," Reimer recalls, adding the job taught him one thing: "I never want to be a fruit farmer."

"But I consider it to be a privilege and an honour to live in a country with wonderful, endless opportunities," he adds.

A builder is born

By the time he was 18, Reimer had already seized another opportunity: The chance to work on residential construction sites during his summer holidays. But he thoroughly enjoyed this work and it would later become a source of solid, full-time employment after he left high school.

As he continued working in construction, Reimer became skilful at building footings and would eventually become knowledgeable in all phases of new home construction, including the design and building of kitchen cabinets.

Becoming an expert

He also studied blue prints and building codes every spare moment he could find.

It wasn't uncommon for Reimer to sit up reading building plans until well after midnight, making himself intimately familiar with every aspect of home construction.

And he became an expert in plumbing, electrical, carpentry, tiling and framing applications and would go on to build more than 2,000 homes – roughing-in at least half of them himself, with help from his carpenters.

While he still just in his teens, Reimer routinely

astonished developers with his intimate knowledge of all matters construction.

More than once, the young worker found himself promoted to foreman after nonchalantly solving a complicated building problem – saving the developer a good deal of money in the process.

"To get ahead in life, sometimes you have to do a little homework," Reimer explains.

"My hobby was learning everything I possibly could about construction – and that's still my hobby," he adds. "For me, business and serving the community my greatest hobby and my greatest challenge."

Going it alone

Reimer was clearly forging impressive success in business – and he then decided to go in business for himself. Starting a construction firm was for Reimer an easy decision: He really enjoyed working on homes.

"In 1954, I worked about a year for a contractor in the Vineland area, doing everything from painting basement walls to laying kitchen tiles," he notes.

"Then a year later, at age 19, I went into business as a subcontractor working for the same contractor," he adds.

"I had 40 people working for me, doing the labour. I was able to do the work at less cost and I doubled the money I was making."

A full-fledged contractor

A year later, Reimer had just turned 20 when he decided to become a full-fledged contractor and built a large house in Grimsby, purely on speculation that once it was built, he'd find a buyer. In fact, a doctor and his new bride soon purchased the luxury dwelling.

Then, Reimer built a second-move-up house for the same doctor.

Buoyed by his success, Reimer continued building homes in the Niagara Peninsula, from Niagara Falls to Hamilton.

"Our motto was to have satisfied customers – which kept us very busy," he recalls with a smile.

Building a better life

"When I was a kid, I never had enough money to buy an ice cream cone, so I was determined to build a better life for my children," Reimer explains.

"So I ended up working seven years straight before I ever took a vacation."

It was also in 1957, when Reimer took the fateful step of becoming a general contractor, taking over the business of a contractor who had retired.

Reimer lacked start up capital. But he did have someone who believed in this ambitious young man.

Robert Johnson, president of the Penn Cashway in Grimsby, had told Reimer he was there to help if Reimer needed his assistance.

"He told me if there was every anything I needed, to contact him," Reimer recalls, "so I went to him and asked him to lend me $250,000."

"Mr. Johnson wrote a cheque for $250,000 and as he handed it to me, he told me it was his retirement money so if I blew it he'd have worked his whole life for nothing," Reimer recollects.

"It was a big responsibility and I wasn't about to let him down. I paid him back in six months with 6 per cent interest."

A builder emerges

Reimer went on to build many homes across Niagara and Hamilton areas, including the homes of prominent doctors and dentists and the Auch Mar neighbourhood on Hamilton Mountain.

Building largely in the Grimsby area, he constructed starter, move-up and retirement homes for repeat customers, enthralled with the quality of workmanship they had found in their starter homes.

By his early twenties, Reimer had already emerged as an up-and-coming builder with a reputation for great workmanship and strict attention to details.

The fatherless war-child had risen from impoverished beginnings and excelled in his new homeland.

He was now in full control of his game.

But this successful young man was about to receive news that would take him by surprise.

"An overwhelming experience"

"I was 16 when we got word that my father was still alive," Reimer says, his eyes widening as he recalls the memory. "It was an overwhelming experience."

In 1962, with help from Vineland's Mennonite congregation, Anna Reimer arranged for a meeting with Russian leader Nikita Khrushchev during his visit that year to the United States.

Khrushchev personally intervened and in a short time, returned Peter Reimer to his family.

Rudy Reimer was 26 when he was reunited with his father, who had spent 18 years in prison.

"I hadn't seen my dad since I was seven years old and I sometimes wondered if he'd been killed," Reimer says, slowly shaking his head.

"It was a very emotional reunion. But it was great to have my dad back after all those years apart."

The experience had a lasting and profound impact on Reimer, who would later become a key player in the Gorbachev Foundation, established by former Soviet Union leader Mikhail Gorbachev to promote world peace and global economic development following the break-up of the USSR.

Meeting world leaders

Reimer has also met and spent time with most of Canada's prime ministers in the past few decades, along with such world leaders as former U.S. presidents George H. Bush and Bill Clinton and former British Prime Minister Margaret Thatcher and the Queen and Queen Mother.

In fact, Clinton wrote him a letter, while in office, thanking Reimer for his thoughts and advice.

And he's served on dozens of boards – including the Hamilton Tiger-Cat Corporate Advisory Board – committees and organizations where he's rubbed shoulders with leading business executives, medical professionals and prominent politicians.

Reimer's experience and understanding of world politics and his business success on a global stage have made him a sought-after source of advice for many businesses and world leaders.

The move to Burlington

By 1961, serviced land had become scarce in the Grimsby area. But Reimer had also started several developments in Burlington, so he made another fateful move and became a highly active builder in Burlington, building the Tyandaga Estates and Ravenswood subdivisions, many North Shore homes and numerous other prestigious dwellings.

Reimer has built homes for many prominent lawyers, doctors and other professional people and executives, including the former chairman of Quebec Hydro, and a former vice-president of Ford Motor Company of Canada.

In particular, Reimer built a number of executive homes in the Tyandaga area, including his own home, a sprawling, palatial mansion.

A 1970 open house drew 12,000 people, police crowd control and a lot of publicity.

In fact, Reimer often moves into one of his homes in the neighbourhoods he builds.

He's lived in 30 houses since age 20 and he often sells his personal homes fully furnished.

His current home features a 3,000-square-foot bedroom, larger than most homes.

Going commercial

In 1972, Reimer had already built more than 2,000 homes when he was encouraged by the City of Burlington to take on commercial development.

He became so successful at this type of development that in 1975, he switched to exclusively developing office and manufacturing buildings.

One of his first, and highly successful Burlington-located commercial projects in the early 1970s was an office and warehousing building at Mainway and Blair Road.

Next was a commercial building holding the Royal Bank, on Harvester Road.

"Burlington is a real business community," Reimer smiles.

"The income level here tends to be better, and many people are either businessmen or they think like businessmen. The whole community takes a very business-like approach to growth and creating success."

Reimer quickly emerged in Burlington as a full-service developer, acquiring the raw land, servicing the site, developing the location, financing and promoting the development and then selling the finished product.

Doing it all

Simply put, he did it all. And still does. He also manages and leases out many of his various commercial complexes.

He usually likes to build for himself and then sell or lease out the space.

In fact, Reimer Construction excels at doing its own land developing, design, building, leasing and decorating – all at competitive rates.

"That's how we still like to do business," Reimer explains. "When you can do the whole thing – you can make more money down the road."

Reimer also credits much of the success of his commercial projects to real estate agents Jim Grieve and John Landry who had worked for him for 30 years. Both men have passed away, but are recalled fondly by Reimer who retains "the highest respect for them."

A New Life

In 1989, Reimer married Teresa Mercer, a native of Georgia.

Prior to getting married, the two planned their dream home together and it took nearly two years to complete the magnificent 15,000-square-foot home.

The bathroom alone is larger than homes he'd lived in as a child in Europe.

"In my life, I've experienced the poorest of accommodations and I've experienced the richest of accommodations," Reimer acknowledges, "and I'm very grateful for the opportunity to achieve success after experiencing poverty."

Teresa Reimer continues to operate T. Reimer Design Consultants Inc.

It's now located in the newest Reimer tower, in an office just down the hall from her husband's office.

In 1990, the newlywed Reimer began building the impressive office towers off Burloak Drive where the penthouse headquarters of Reimer Construction were previously located. Many buildings are sold to investors while he continues to manage the complexes.

A Major Commercial Developer

By the early 1990s, Reimer had built more than 1-million square feet of commercial space in impressive glass towers seen throughout Burlington, but especially along the Queen Elizabeth Way.

These developments include Burloak Park on the Oakville border, consisting of a seven-storey tower, a new five-storey tower and research centres.

Twelve acres of this 100-acre site were sold to the Royal Bank of Canada for its Ontario headquarters.

He's also built a convention centre in the Burloak Business Park that seats 900 people. It features three main halls and two boardrooms.

Occupancy took place in 2000 and there were immediate bookings for conventions before the project was even completed.

In early 2002, Reimer completed building a modern, state-of-the-art, 11-storey, 200,000-square-foot, glass tower.

Burlington's most modern building

It's regarded as Burlington's most modern, energy-efficient building. The impressive structure also houses the new headquarters of Reimer Construction. Reimer's wife Teresa's T. Reimer Design company and his son Rudy's R. K. Reimer Developments Limited are also located here.

Reimer has leased out 50 per cent of the space in the newly completed office tower and has drawn major corporations – including General Electric Co. and International Truck and Engine Co. – as tenants.

Other major corporations that have, at one time or another, made their home in a Reimer building, include: Bank of Montreal, Canadian Imperial Bank of Commerce, TD Bank, Trebor Allen candy company,

AIG Life, National Bank, Brinks Security; CUMIS, John Deere, London Life, the Bailey Controls company, Zenon Environmental and Shaklee Canada Ltd.

Beyond commercial development, Reimer has also made his presence felt on the religion front: He purchased the land for the elaborate Park Bible Church and Crossroads development, the home of the television show 100 Huntley Street.

New Project

And there's a new project in the works: On the Reimers' return from a trip to Spain in the summer of 2002, the couple brought back some more ideas that may lead to another major project.

Reimer is planning to build the largest commercial complex in Burlington.

He's already dubbed the elaborate structure 'The Palace'.

And he's now actively contemplating constructing the complex at a location just off South Service Road in Burlington.

The trip to Spain inspired Reimer to come up with the proposed 300,000-square-foot complex, loosely based on the Westin Palace hotel in Madrid.

He hopes to start in on construction of the project in early 2003 and is already contemplating eventually relocating his head office to the proposed new, 12-storey structure, which is to feature high ceilings, elegant columns and a soaring rooftop dome and skylight.

The new commercial complex will also hold a convention centre, which is not expected to be any competition problem for the existing business park's convention facilities as there is currently no shortage of people interested in leasing space at the facilities for an array of upcoming scheduled events.

Numerous awards

Reimer's exemplary work in Burlington has earned him more than 30 awards and citations of merit, including the prestigious and first-ever ***Lifetime Achievement Award*** from the Burlington Chamber of Commerce.

Of course he more recently won the prestigious ***Queen's Golden Jubilee Medal*** recognizing his very "significant contribution," to Canada and Canadians.

There's also his ***Commemorative Medal*** from the Governor General and his listing in the Who's Who's National Register among the most prominent North American executives and top professionals.

Reimer Construction was also a finalist for the international Prix Excellence Awards, emerging in the top 22 of competing companies from 145 countries around the world.

Over the years, Reimer has donated to various charities, hospitals and worthy causes, endlessly giving back to the community.

Reimer attributes his company's enduring success to his staff, his investors, his tenants and the people who have believed in him and supported his career in one way or another over the years

"I think one of the reasons we've been successful is that we always try to exceed the expectations of our investors, our tenants and everyone who does business with us," he explains. "People don't realize how easy it is to make money – all you have to do is satisfy your customer."

Adding value

One way Reimer keeps his customers happy is by adding value to his work while also minimizing his costs: Instead of spending $200,000 on architectural fees from the concept stage onward, Reimer initially envisions the building and then personally creates a rough sketch.

That sketch is then turned over to son Rudy for elaboration and added details.

Only after that point are the plans finally turned over to an architect for finalizing formal blueprints.

Doing it all

By only bringing a professional architect into the process when he's absolutely needed, Reimer cuts substantial costs.

This allows him to reinvest the savings in other areas, such as interior decorating, which is controlled by Teresa Reimer.

The buildings offer panoramic views with expensive triple-pane glass – but energy savings more than overcomes this cost.

Energy savings are also achieved through long-lasting lighting.

Rather than hire a negotiator, Reimer's son Rudy K. Reimer does his own negotiating with all trades people.

Reimer's wife Teresa adds incredible value to the building interiors through her design work.

Many building interiors are of marble and expensive woods.

Elevators often feature built-in small television sets. Plants, trees, flowers and decorative touches are everywhere.

Great value for dollars spent

The result of cost-cutting, quality-enhancing efforts is to provide premium, luxury office space to tenants at a bargain rate: Often a highly competitive $25-per-square-foot of gross rent.

"We stay within practical limitations of what our customers can afford and what we save on architects, we spend on decorating, to give the customer the most value at a fairly low rate," Reimer explains.

"We say that for $25 per square foot, you won't find better value than what we're offering."

Although hard work is an important part of Reimer's success strategy, it's only one component.

"I've seen too many hard-working people who are very poor," he says.

"It's important not just to work hard, but to work smart as well, to cut unnecessary costs and add value to really please your customers," Reimer notes.

"If you can find ways to work smart and make all of your customers happy, you'll earn many referrals and get a lot of repeat busines," he adds.

"Treating your customers well will help make you become very successful today, tomorrow and well into the future."

Rudy Reimer's tips for success:

1. Do your homework when you take on a new job or business. Learn all you can about the work involved so you can increase your expertise and gain new skills.

2. Hire the best people you can find and keep them motivated and contributing their skills to your endeavours. Make sure they understand their efforts are appreciated.

3. Do as much work as you can in-house, contracting out only the most necessary tasks to experienced outside consultants.

4. Know your limitations. While you should keep most work in-house, make sure you do not go beyond your expertise. It can save money to bring in a consultant as needed.

5. Work hard – but also work smart. Hard work alone won't earn success. You should always work as efficiently as possible.

6. Learn to delegate. Part of working smarter means letting others perform routine tasks.

7. Know your market. Develop a business plan and do some research to determine who and where your customers are.

8. Provide the best value you can at a good price and deliver what you promise.

9. Make your customers happy. In addition to providing the customer good value, throw in unexpected extras that will draw a smile.

10. Network. Your customers and suppliers are good sources for putting you in touch with other potential customers through referrals.

11. Find the lowest cost, best way of providing your goods or services and pass some of the savings on to the customer, either in the form of reduced costs or enhanced value.

12. Be prepared to put in long hours while building your firm into a successful entity.

13. No matter how busy you get with business, always allow time for your loved ones – and reward yourself and your family when your business starts to succeed.

14. Make sure that whatever your business endeavour is, it's something you truly enjoy being involved with: Your work should be an enjoyable challenge – not a chore – and it should be beneficial to your community.

15. As you build your company, make sure you contribute to your community, your religion and charity as a prosperous community also makes for successful people.

Teresa Reimer

Chapter Three

Teresa Reimer

Success by design

"We include decorative columns, mirrors and woodwork to achieve an interesting and formal yet warm look. I like what can best be described as a neo-classical look using pillars and marble – it's a blend of classical and modern influences,"
- **Teresa Reimer**

At a Glance: Teresa Reimer
and T. Reimer Design Consultants Inc.

Teresa Reimer
Age: 39
Title: President, T. Reimer Design Consultants Inc.
Claim to fame: Performs outstanding and imaginative interior design work for clients, with most of her talent dedicated to the interiors of buildings developed by husband Rudy P. Reimer. She's the 2002-2003 President of the Junior League of Hamilton-Burlington Inc. and is a board member of the Hamilton Philharmonic Orchestra. With her husband, she supports many charities.
Financial Data: Undisclosed. Private Company.
Personal: Resides in Burlington with husband Rudy P. Reimer in a dream house the couple planned out together.
For More information:
Contact: T. Reimer Design Consultants Inc.:
(905) 336-8775
Fax: (905) 336-7936.
Address: 9th Floor, Reimer Millennium Tower, 5500 North Service Road, Burlington, Ontario, L7L 6W6.
email: treimer@sympatico.ca

Chapter Three
Teresa Reimer
Designed To Succeed

Teresa Reimer takes pride in improving the world around her.

As the president of T. Reimer Design Consultants Inc., Reimer enjoys transforming cold corporate spaces into warm inviting places.

And as 2002-2003 president of the Junior League of Hamilton-Burlington Inc., Reimer has also spent the past dozen years supporting charitable works, improving the lives of countless people.

She also works tirelessly on many charitable ventures with her husband, Rudy P. Reimer.

"Every year, Rudy has a crusade and he's great at promoting a cause and supporting it, while I like doing a lot of the behind-the-scenes work," she explains in an interview at her elegant, ninth floor office in one of the newer, 11-storey, glass towers built by Reimer Construction.

"We make a great team," adds Reimer, 39, surveying the panoramic view from her office in a 230,000-square-foot building situated in the 100-acre Burloak Business Park, opposite Bronte Provincial Park at the Burlington-Oakville border.

Together with her husband, Teresa Reimer has become a positive force in the Burlington area. She has a well-earned reputation as a caring woman who has made a major difference in the community.

How this ardent Junior Leaguer came to run her own interior decorating company, marry a prominent developer and devote so much of her time to helping others is a story that begins in the American State of Georgia.

A Southern Belle's Story

Teresa was born in Atlanta, Georgia, the only daughter and eldest child of Inge and the late Walter Mercer. The Mercers also had a son, William, one year Teresa's junior.

After a happy childhood in Atlanta, she enrolled at Georgia State University where she majored in Marketing and earned a BBA degree.

In 1981, early into her program, she embarked on a cruise – a high school graduation gift from her parents. It was a voyage that would forever change the life of the tall and attractive, slender, young blonde.

While wandering around the crowded cruise ship, she happened upon Rudy Reimer, a Canadian businessman travelling solo and trying his luck at the ship's gaming tables.

"I was just standing there," she recalls with a grin, "and I could see he wasn't having much luck. He threw down some chips and asked me to play for him – he forced me to gamble."

"So I did play," she continues, "and I doubled his money. I gave him back his original $100 and kept the winnings and walked away. At the end of the cruise, I saw him again on the dock and he asked for my address, so I wrote it down and drew a happy face on the note – I honestly thought I'd never see him again."

Later, he sent flowers, which prompted her to telephone her thanks.

"Rudy told me years later he thought the smiley face I'd drawn had some deeper meaning," Reimer recalls. "I find it very touching that he kept it for over 20 years. One day he pulled it out of his wallet to show it to me. He carries it like a talisman."

"It's Got To Be Love"

"It was amazing," she recalls. "He sent me flowers every second week for a long time – he spent thousands of dollars a year just on flowers. And I always called to thank him and we'd talk, but for the first few years, I only actually saw him twice. And he actually talked more to my mom than me, as I wasn't home much. He'd send flowers and tape recordings he made to let me know how he was doing and what he was up to. I didn't know any guy my age that would go to such extremes, so I thought it's got to be love. He was so persistent."

She says the flowers also had the effect of chasing away any would-be suitors at the college.

"Getting those flowers every other week while I was living on campus kept the other guys away because they assumed I had a steady boyfriend – I figure now that was his strategy," she smiles.

"After graduating from university I became even more interested in him. I went from just thinking he was a nice guy, to falling in love with him. I realized we're soul-mates and that this is the guy I'll spend the rest of my life with."

She moved to Burlington in 1989 and began doing interior design work for Reimer Construction, founding her own company two years later.

The couple began making wedding plans and married in 1989 after first planning their 15,000-square-foot dream home together. She would later hold house tours at her own home and other large area homes to raise funds for charity. The events drew upwards of 7,000 people and raised many tens of thousands of dollars.

Dubbed 'The Plantation' the Reimer mansion near Guelph Line in Burlington has a master bedroom that boasts 3,000 square feet of space and the bathroom is a full 50-feet-long.

"You want to make sure you really have to use the bathroom, because it's a bit of hike getting there," Reimer laughs.

Of course, if they really want to go on a hike, the couple need only stroll around the exterior of their home 10 times to have walked a full mile.

Understated Opulence

In fact, Reimer has a proven knack for creating powerful yet warm decors that are infused with an understated opulence.

"I've always liked decorating and I found I had a knack for it," notes Reimer who was initially a salaried employee of Reimer Construction, serving as the company's in-house design consultant.

The in-house work soon led to Reimer starting her own independent firm with Reimer Construction as its biggest single customer.

"We include decorative columns, mirrors and woodwork to achieve an interesting and formal yet warm look," she explains.

"I like what can best be described as a neo-classical look using pillars and marble – it's a blend of classical and modern influences," she adds.

Although she occasionally performs contract work outside of Reimer Construction, most of Teresa Reimer's interior design work remains focused on the prestige commercial complexes owned and/or managed by her husband.

"It's more than enough to keep me very busy," Reimer says with a laugh.

"After all," she adds, "we've got more than a million square feet of space to see to in 20 buildings with 110 tenants. And there are often new tenants moving into our buildings."

"I also enjoy listening to our tenants and helping them out by meeting their needs," she adds.

"Rudy provided me with some seed money to help get me going and he provides the office space, receptionist and staff so I really have no overhead of my own."

A Great Team

"My husband is the mastermind behind all of this," Reimer says, spreading her arms as if to take in all of the many commercial complexes that comprise Reimer Country and beyond.

"Rudy is the entrepreneur with the vision," she adds. "He's very energetic. He's certainly got more energy than I do. When he sets his mind on something, there's no stopping him. Rudy will never retire because he loves doing business deals, and he's very gutsy – I admire that about him."

Reimer says she and her husband bring out the best in each other "and we've found that we're perfectly matched for each other – we really do make a great team. A lot of people won't believe this, but Rudy used to be shy – but I brought that out of him."

Keeping husband youthful

"I make him young – and he ages me," she says, suppressing a giggle. "Life with Rudy is a labour of love – with an emphasis on the labour," she adds with a snicker.

All joking aside, Reimer describes her marriage as "really, really great," adding life with the dynamic developer has also meant meeting many celebrated world figures, including former U.S. President Bill Clinton, who struck her as "charming, charismatic, graceful and brilliant," former Prime Minister Brian Mulroney and wife Mila and the late Queen Mother.

Reimer enjoys making travel arrangements on behalf of herself and her husband – "I plan it out and look after all the details" – and the couple enjoys spending two to three months a year visiting other countries. To keep memories of the trips fresh and alive, Reimer takes numerous photographs and keeps photo albums and scrapbooks.

"I'll never forget the butterfly garden in Singapore," Reimer smiles. "And last year, we went to Africa – my dream trip. This year it's Australia and Spain. We love travelling. Rudy picks up ideas about building and I sometimes come away with some design ideas."

Dedicated To The Junior League

Reimer estimates spending 50 hours a week on her business and another 20 hours per week on Junior League, an organization she's been devoted to for the past dozen years.

During her first two years with the Junior League, Reimer sat on the design committee for Ronald McDonald House in Hamilton and helped raise $250,000 in gifts-in-kind.

The Junior League is currently focused on a capital campaign for Grace Haven, a centre for pregnant adolescents, women and young single parents. Programs are available on a residential and community basis. Services include a high school program, clothing exchange, parenting skills development, counselling and life skills training.

"In my 11 years with the Junior League of Hamilton-Burlington, we've distributed more than $490,000 to our local communities," Reimer notes. "These purposeful grants and disbursements allow our organization to make a positive difference."

Founded a century ago in the United States, the Junior League organization now boasts 296 League groups in 45 countries.

There are eight leagues in Canada. In addition to Hamilton-Burlington – which has 200 members – locations include Montreal, Halifax, Toronto, Calgary, Edmonton, Winnipeg and Vancouver. All Canadian leagues are affiliated with the U.S.-based organization. Reimer says her involvement with Junior League has helped her develop organizational/ managerial skills.

"The women in the league never cease to amaze me with their dedication, commitment and enthusiasm, along with the great skills they bring to the process," Reimer smiles.

Giving Back

For eight years straight, Reimer also put on puppet shows with four-foot-tall puppets to teach children at dozens of schools about social issues such as vandalism. Puppet skits were also used to address and increase awareness of disabilities ranging from asthma to leukemia, diabetes, blindness, deafness and cerebral palsy.

"Another nice thing about my Junior League involvement is that I've met and gotten to know so many interesting, talented and inspiring women," Reimer notes.

Junior League has approximately 192,000 female members worldwide. The League was established to give women the opportunity to contribute their skill sets to worthy causes. Among the League's prominent former members is Laura Bush, wife of U.S. President George W. Bush.

"Basically we draw from the talents of successful women who volunteer their expertise – in anything from accounting to legal work or artistic or marketing skills – to projects we elect to support," Reimer notes.

"Junior League participation is a great way to give back to your community," she adds.
"There's a lot of satisfaction in helping others."

Teresa Reimer's tips for success:

1. Play to your strengths. Find something that you like doing and that you're good at doing – then excel in this endeavour.

2. Form alliances with others (for example: Junior League) as this can bring in additional skills.

3. Be prepared to put in long hours. But invest your time wisely to achieve your goals.

4. Learn not only to develop your own talents but also those of others. Try to bring out the best in yourself and everyone around you.

5. Go beyond merely satisfying your customer. Delight your clients by going the extra mile to deliver impressive added touches.

6. Support charities and worthy causes. You can make a difference. Giving back to your community can be very satisfying.

7. Praise staff for good work. This rewards and encourages more great performances.

8. Organize your time. There's a lot you can achieve if you focus on the important tasks at hand and not become distracted.

9. Listen to your customers. Find out what they want and try to meet their needs.

10. Do business in an honest and forthright manner – and grow through many referrals.

Rudy K. Reimer

Chapter Four

Rudy K. Reimer

Watching The Rising Son

"My father will often come up with a concept and design and he'll do a feasibility study. Then, I'll fine tune the design and make sure it's cost-effective and that the layout is functional. I'll improve the design if necessary and build the best project possible… If we build it, they will come."

- **Rudy K. Reimer**

At a Glance: Rudy K. Reimer and R. K. Reimer Developments:

Rudy K. Reimer
Age: 44
Title: President R. K. Reimer Developments Limited.
Claim to fame: Major developer of commercial buildings. Tenants read like a Who's Who of International business leaders. With his father, Rudy Reimer Sr., he's changing Burlington's skyline and turning the city into a major commercial centre.
Financial Data: Largely undisclosed. However, this is a successful company, growing steadily.
Personal: Resides in Burlington with wife Jan. The couple welcomed the arrival of their first child, Brittany, in the spring of 2002. He's the only son of Rudy Reimer Sr. and has a sister, Darlene. He's also a private pilot who enjoys flying and traveling.
For More information:
Contact: R. K. Reimer Developments Limited: (905) 336-8775
Fax: (905) 336-7936.
Address: 9th Floor, Reimer Millennium Tower, 5500 North Service Road, Burlington, Ontario, L7L 6W6.
Email: rkreimer@sympatico.ca

Chapter Four

Rudy K. Reimer

Watching The Rising Son

"If we build it, they will come," Rudy K. Reimer says with a smile.

"That's our philosophy," adds the president of R. K. Reimer Developments Limited as he surveys an impressive view of glass towers at Burloak Park in the heart of Reimer Country.

And it seems that whatever Reimer builds, there are plenty of prospective tenants eager to move into his impressive commercial buildings.

It helps that he knows all the angles.

"I don't think we've ever built a true square building – they're all asymmetrical in design," notes Reimer, 44, gazing through an angled window at a panoramic view of Burlington, Hamilton, Lake Ontario and the Niagara Escarpment.

"The more angles you have, the more views

you can have," he explains. "It makes for a more conversational architecture. A square building only has four corners per floor for the executive suites, whereas an irregular shape provides for many more."

Indeed, Reimer and his company are known for the exacting standards they apply to building construction.

Lasers are routinely used to establish precise angles and the buildings, always designed to feature a number of angles, afford many great views.

Reimer established his company in 1979 and it has gone on to achieve considerable success in the ensuing decades.

The company does projects on behalf of Reimer Construction along with its own projects. It also does all of the property management for all the Reimer buildings.

Successful Company

"We'll keep on moving forward – we've got a good thing going – our staff and our trades people are behind us, helping us earn success," he notes.

"We'll sell our buildings or turn over the management to others – providing we're confident the tenants will receive an equal level of quality or property management that would be to industry standards," Reimer notes.

"Our property management portfolio is something we don't want to contract out as we could lose the personal touch we provide," Reimer points out.

"Our success has been built on the personal contact and services we give to our tenants. Our goal is leasing space – still the most profitable – but the management side is still very important to us and it always will be."

Reimer says tenants have come to appreciate the company's hands-on approach and willingness to make leased space feel like home.

"The personal touch we provide has helped fuel the company's growth – and I enjoy the work. It's fun building. Every day it's something new. We're changing the landscape, building something new. It's a great way to get some fresh air in the summer, and stay warm inside during the winter."

In addition to building, Reimer, a private pilot, also enjoys flying every chance he gets. He also enjoys landscaping, his new daughter, astronomy and evenings out with friends.

Studies market conditions

Before a building project is undertaken, the company studies market conditions and then determines the project's feasibility and likelihood, in the given environment, of attracting enough 'triple-A' tenants.

If conditions are viewed as favourable by his company's standards, the company will build the structure and then lease out the space, and manage the property.

"Our standard of a good economic climate is different than others," Reimer states. "We have always found it better to construct in a poor economy rather than a robust season."

Reimer's key role – one he excels at – is to add value to concepts his father envisions and then help make each project a reality by taking a very practical, cost-efficient approach to construction.

"My father will often come up with a concept and design and he'll do a feasibility study and give me a rough sketch of what he has in mind," Reimer explains.

"Then, I'll fine tune the design and make sure it's cost-effective and that the layout is functional and is workable in terms of building codes, fire codes and zoning," he adds.

Savings reinvested in improvements

"I'll improve the practicality on paper, if necessary, then we'll finally bring in our architect to add the final touches," Reimer says, noting that limiting the architect's contracted involvement in the overall process can generate substantial cost savings, which can transferred on to other building improvements, giving tenants superb space at highly competitive rates.

"By the time we go to the architect, the concept is fully in place – and it's all been done in house. We've already priced the building and completed our budget."

"We pre-plan but avoid any excessive over-planning. We get involved with our trades people on a regular basis and co-ordinate their input and expertise. We're constantly learning new ways to improve efficiencies," he adds.

"The bottom line is: We have the expertise to build in the most economical and safest manner possible – and we'll build the best project possible," Reimer asserts.

"We know what we want and our approach streamlines the whole process without cutting any corners. We'll more than meet all codes, standards and building guidelines."

Reimer admits the company's approach is "a little unique in our methodology – we tend to do our fine-tuning first, and the bulk of construction, last. This is unorthodox to most methods, but it helps us to eliminate additional expenditures up front, rather than later."

"It's the way we've always done business and it's worked well for us – we continue to be successful in the projects we take on, and I see this pattern continuing for some time to come," he adds.

Skilled Trades Shortage Concern

However, one concern Reimer sees on the looming construction horizon is a coming shortage of young skilled trades people to replace the older generation.

"Most of our trades men are middle-aged and older," Reimer notes, "and there really isn't anyone out there to replace them."

"What we're always looking for are skilled trades people who will have the necessary skills and pride in their work to satisfactorily replace the highly skilled and dedicated older trades people we have now," he asserts.

"Unfortunately, the trades usually aren't a young person's first choice for an occupation – but there's no good reason for that. These are good, well-paying jobs that need to be filled," he adds.

"The days are long gone when we could look to immigrants from Europe to fill those skilled trades jobs.

The post-war boom to "make a new life in America," and the ethnical Baby Boomers associated with it, have subsided substantially."

Reimer says today's youth should seriously consider skilled trades work as a satisfying and well-paying way to make a living.

Born To Build

And Reimer knows what it means to embrace the construction industry at a young age.

Although he was born the son of a successful developer, there were still no shortcuts for Rudy K. Reimer.

In fact, his rise to success literally began at ground level.

"I started out in the construction business pushing a broom during summers and after school," Reimer recalls with a smile. "I was about nine years old and being a little guy, I was just the right size for sweeping out low-headroom crawl spaces in the homes my dad built."

"Then I graduated to cleaning out whole houses – I still hold the record for the most homes cleaned in one day," he chuckles.

"When I got a little older, I was paid $6-a-lawn to cut the grass at my father's housing developments."

"Then I realized I could make better use of my time and still make a buck so I subcontracted the work out and paid my friends $3-a-lawn."

That may have been the first entrepreneurial spark from Reimer. But it wouldn't be the last from a developer who has achieved an enviable degree of success on his own.

His firm is completely independent of Reimer Construction and has earned a reputation as a leading developer.

Indeed, strict attention to details and a desire to add value and exceed expectations are common threads tying Rudy K. Reimer's company and the various Reimer Country companies together.

With such laudable shared values in place, these independent companies are well positioned to take on and conquer any and all challenges they may encounter as we move deeper into the new millennium.

As a youngster growing up in Burlington, Rudy K. Reimer had the advantage of being more focused than most of his peers.

"I always knew I'd be in the family business and I tended to concentrate more on that than on my schoolwork at times," he recalls.

"At age ten, I would reproduce front and rear elevations of our homes from the 'sight-to-paper' method, with good accuracy," he adds.

"By Grade 12, I knew a lot more about framing houses than math. But this is a constant learning experience and I later became good at math because I use it in building."

Gateway To Burlington

And he does a lot of building. The newest project on stream is a 300,000-square-foot office complex complete with retail space and a new convention centre, planned for a South Service Road location.

"This is the business hub for all of Burlington,

it's its own commercial centre, also known as Reimer Country," he states.

"We now have well over 100 major tenants here, including the Burlington Convention Centre, which act as magnets for bringing other business people to this area," he notes.

"This area has become a catalyst for growth and has helped fuel the city's infrastructure potential," he adds.

"We continue to believe that Burlington is the place to be – and we're proud to be playing a role in the city's development as a major commercial centre."

Rudy K. Reimer's tips for success:

1. Always set a goal for yourself, whether it's profit oriented, or otherwise. It's important that you should always try to do whatever it is you like to do.

2. Be efficient with your time. Time is of the essence – use it wisely.

3. Try to excel in school. You may not like certain subjects – such as math – but you may need these subjects in the working world.

4. Respect your employees and people you work with. You can't do everything by yourself. You'll need the help of other people, so treat them well.

5. Learn to delegate. It makes more sense to assign day-to-day tasks to others to free up you time. Time is of the essence.

6. Build, and maintain, a personal touch with clients. Nurturing a business relationship can mean repeat business and referrals that will help you company grow.

7. Take pride in your work. If you're pleased with the job you've done, others will feel the same way.

8. Treat your business as a constant learning experience. Never accept that you know it all, because you don't. Build your knowledge base.

9. Enjoy what you do. Your business should also be your hobby. When it's no longer fun to do, it just becomes work. Once it's just work, it's only a job that you don't enjoy. To remain motivated and be successful, you should derive a sense of satisfaction from your work.

10. Be persistent and assertive and always do what you say you're going to do. Don't be intimidated by anyone. You should always believe you're as good or better than the other guy. Have confidence in yourself and don't put yourself down.

Sue DePaulo

Chapter Five

Sue DePaulo

Turning Houses Into Homes

"I want the clients to really, truly love the property they're buying and I don't feel right unless they feel it's the perfect home for them."

- Sue DePaulo

At a Glance: Sue DePaulo and Royal LePage State Realty:

Sue DePaulo
Age: 47
Title: Sales Representative, Royal LePage State Realty in Ancaster, an independently owned and operated broker in the Royal LePage organization.

Claim to fame: A former banker turned top-selling real estate agent for much of the past decade. DePaulo specializes in providing personal service and is very attentive to her clients' needs. She also possesses terrific communication skills and maintains close contact with clients at all times. Her caring, thorough approach and strict attention to details have earned her numerous referrals.

Personal: Born and raised in Dundas. Now resides in Ancaster with husband Gary, 51; and their three children: Mark, 21; Michael, 19; and Marissa, 13.

For More information:
Contact: Sue DePaulo, Royal LePage State Realty:
Phone: (905) 648-4451 or (905) 525-3737.
FAX: (905) 648-7393.
Address: 51 Wilson Street West, Ancaster, Ontario, L9G 1N1 (next to Shoppers Drug Mart in the Food Basics plaza).
Email: suedepaulo@royallepage.ca
Website: www.royallepage.ca

Chapter Five

Sue DePaulo
Turning Houses Into Homes

Choosing Sue DePaulo as your real estate agent guarantees two things.

One: You've made a great choice: Sue DePaulo is a dedicated, award-winning agent.

Two: You're going to see a lot of her.

"I like spending a lot of time with my clients," DePaulo acknowledges during an interview at her executive home in Ancaster, where she's answering questions between phone calls and getting ready for another appointment in an already hectic day that's only just started.

"It's time well-spent as it helps you gain an appreciation of the clients' needs and wants," adds DePaulo, noting she often logs 30 hours per month just on her cell phone, "and time spent on land phones and meeting clients is in addition to that."

DePaulo also asserts that she doesn't feel she's done her job unless she finds a home that's "not only the type of home the client is looking for, but a home that will really make them happy,"

For example, DePaulo recalls one of many cases in which she'd spent many weeks taking a client around to see houses and finally found one that met all the criteria.

"I found a property that was everything my client said she was looking for – but she didn't seem that thrilled or excited about it," DePaulo recollects.

"I knew it wasn't for her, so I persuaded her not to buy it."

Making sure clients are happy

Having succeeded in not making the sale, DePaulo then went on to prove she is in fact a very good sales agent.

She continued the search and found the home of her client's dreams.

"My client was very grateful – and happy," beams DePaulo, who has built her business on referrals from that satisfied customer and many others like her.

The fact that finding the perfect right home – as opposed to finding a home that was adequate – meant putting in a lot of extra hours didn't faze DePaulo at all.

"It just comes with the territory," she says with a laugh.

"I want the clients to really love the property they're buying and I don't feel right unless they feel it's the perfect home for them," she explains.

"My approach is one of no pressure and I'm very patient and quite willing to show dozens of houses until we find the right one," she adds.

"Who cares if it takes a little longer? I don't just want to make a sale, I want to make a sale that makes the client happy," DePaulo asserts.

"And it takes time," she says.

"I could never just do this job part-time as I once originally thought, because I think you have to be really dedicated to serving your clients," DePaulo adds with a smile.

"I find that it's all or nothing. So I always give it my all."

A lot of time spent with clients

This laudable approach of always making her clients her top priority means a lot of extra work – and a lot of extra time spent with the client.

And it's personal time.

"I know some agents delegate some things to others and I'm not knocking them – we each have our own approach," DePaulo states.

"But I rarely delegate anything because my approach is very hands-on and I like to personally deal with clients," she explains.

"I like to personally handle open houses, house showings and home searches," she adds, noting she bypasses the secretarial service to personally make her own appointments.

"My handling most of my calls personally means more to the client, I feel, and I know it's really appreciated – most of my business is through referrals."

"I'm the only one who spends time with my clients, other than my husband Gary, who assists me," she explains.

"I like to do everything myself, and I try not to carry more than a dozen listings at any one time, because I wouldn't feel comfortable trying to juggle them all," she says.

"I'm happier with fewer listings because I can give more personal service to clients," she adds.

"That's just the way I am."

Her clients appreciate her personal touch.

"It's a very satisfying and rewarding job because people really appreciate the dedication, the amount of work involved and the many hours I put in on their behalf," DePaulo smiles.

"If I'm known for anything, it's the personal attention I give my clients – I'm known for babying my clients," she admits with a chuckle.

Sue DePaulo Withdrawal

In fact, one client so enjoyed the time spent with DePaulo that the client expressed her regrets after her house sold and the two inevitably had less contact with each other.

"I miss our daily conversations," the client wrote. "I'm having Sue DePaulo withdrawal!"

DePaulo chuckles when reminded of that comment, and then admits that she sometimes phones former clients at their request "just to chat – we'll really miss each other after we've spent so much time together."

Unfortunately, "Sue DePaulo withdrawal" is a risk many clients take when they use the services of this cheerful, bubbly, thoughtful and conscientious sales representative.

It's clear clients are pleased with her consistent willingness to go the extra mile to make them happy with their real estate experience.

In fact, many of DePaulo's appreciative clients have expressed their gratitude in letters.

"One of the greatest pleasures in my career in real estate is receiving the letters of thanks and the referrals from clients," smiles DePaulo, who has proudly preserved such letters in an album.

Many letters from satisfied clients

Here's just a sampling of excerpts from the many testimonial letters DePaulo has received (last names withheld to respect privacy) over the years:

"Our house was listed for only four weeks before it sold… quite impressive given the relatively slow market… hard-working, professional approach to real estate," – Rick and Debbie, March 1992.

"Thank you for your assistance and advice in making everything possible and mutually satisfying. Your diplomacy and sensitivity are genuinely appreciated… You went far beyond the call of duty." – Pat, April 1993.

"… hard work and dedicated effort… true professionalism," – Kevin, May 1994.

"... a privilege to have had you as our agent,"
– Jim and Diane, December 1995.

DePaulo is proud, if a little embarrassed, on revisiting a scrapbook full of glowing letters of praise.

"But you know," she allows, "it is so nice when people do write to say how much they appreciate what I've done and how pleased they are."

"I live and work by the Golden Rule – I treat people the way I myself would like to be treated," she asserts.

"And for me, that means making the client the priority and always maintaining continual communication with them."

...and more letters of praise

That approach is clearly having an impact. Here are a few more excerpts from the many letters she's received:

"I have never come across an agent that works as hard... dedicated commitment to her clients and her motivational enthusiasm... highly recommend Sue DePaulo to anyone considering buying or selling their home..." – Ernie and Elaine, June 1995.

"... expertise and market awareness created the environment for a quick and favourable sale of our property... professionalism, honesty and knowledge..." – Mary and Bob, June 1995.

"...our sincere appreciation for all your time, dedication and effort... experience and advice... professional while showing concern for our personal needs... understanding," – Dave and Jeanette, August, 1997.

"...helpful, informative, no pressure – and very hard-working..." – Heather and Ted, October 1997.

"... very impressed with your professional approach and friendly manner... took the time to phone us often... prompt feedback... We were very glad to have you on our side in the negotiation of the final price and conditions of sale, with your years of experience in real estate, and your firm but pleasant approach," – Bernd and Vanessa, December 2000.

In addition to drawing rave reviews from clients, DePaulo is also well respected by her colleagues in the real estate industry who often comment that they find her to be very professional.

This praise joins a seemingly endless stream of accolades and awards DePaulo has received over the years, including her selection for cover treatment in Profiles of Success Magazine.

DePaulo's inclusion in the prestigious magazine came after numerous brokers cited her name when asked who was the best representative for their profession both in terms of sales and in terms of individual character.

Consistently top sales agent

In fact, she's consistently been the top sales agent almost every year for the past decade at her office where she works with approximately 40 other real estate agents.

How DePaulo rose to become such a highly successful real estate sales representative is a story that begins in Dundas, the picturesque valley town, now part of the amalgamated city of Hamilton.

Born and raised in Dundas, DePaulo attended Cathedral Girls High School in Hamilton and took Grade 13 at St. Mary's High School, graduating from St. Mary's in 1973.

DePaulo took a year off after graduation to do some travelling, then enrolled at Hamilton's McMaster University to pursue a Bachelor degree in psychology.

In 1975, after a year of fulltime studies, she switched to part-time course to begin working as a teller for the Toronto Dominion Bank branch at King Street East and Wentworth Street in Hamilton.

Although juggling a fulltime job and part-time studies, DePaulo earned a three-year BA in Psychology in just four years, graduating in 1978.

Began as a banker

During her university years, she continued working at TD, moving up to business accounts manager and then personal loans and mortgages officer.

And during this time, she also married and completed numerous in-branch financial courses.

The couple settled in a quiet Dundas neighbourhood and began preparing for a family.

Although she was, without question, a very successful banker, her husband Gary thought her people skills and communication skills would also make her an excellent real estate agent.

"I've always felt Sue would be great at real estate," Gary DePaulo confirms. "She works hard and she has a way with people."

And he remembers suggesting this career path for his industrious wife on several occasions.

However, DePaulo was quite content with banking, a job she managed to maintain after their first-born child Mark – now 21 – came along.

"I enjoyed the work – I really thought I'd retire there," DePaulo recalls.

Banking career hits unexpected snag

But this manageable situation changed in 1983 with the arrival of their second child, Michael, now 19.

"My second child had some health problems and he was separated from me at birth in order to deal with them," DePaulo recollects.

"I think that because we were apart and didn't go through the usual bonding process, Michael became very clingy as a baby," she surmises, shaking her head on recalling this memory.

"He was fine as long as I was with him," DePaulo recollects.

"But the moment I'd leave the room, he'd start screaming and wouldn't stop."

When her maternity leave ended, DePaulo tried to deal with the situation by bringing in babysitters while she went back to work at the bank.

"But Michael would scream all day long, from the moment I left until the moment I returned," DePaulo recalls.

"We went through five babysitters without success and we decided to change our priorities."

Briefly became stay-at-home mom

DePaulo says she and her husband then decided that she should quit work and stay home while he supported the family on his skilled tradesman's income.

"At that time, Michael needed me to be with him – and I felt that was more important than my career," DePaulo recalls.

She stayed home from early 1984 to late 1985 when the family moved from Dundas to their home in Ancaster, where they still reside to this day.

Shortly after arriving in Ancaster, DePaulo started working part-time for the local Canada Trust branch where they had obtained the mortgage for their home.

"They offered me a part-time job in customer service that still allowed me to spend a lot of time at home," DePaulo recollects.

Real estate career again suggested

While DePaulo continued working a few years with the trust branch, her husband again suggested several times that she go into real estate.

"I thought she's be really good at it," he recalls. "She's got great business skills and people skills."

Instead, DePaulo applied to Teacher's College. Unfortunately, there were many applicants and few positions that particular year so she didn't get in.

Once again, her husband suggested giving real estate a try.

This time, she was ready to consider this major change in career paths.

"My husband kept mentioning this, again and again," DePaulo recalls, "and I finally thought: Why not give it try?"

DePaulo decided to start taking real estate courses in 1988.

The following year, her daughter Marissa, now 13, was born and DePaulo took a year off to spend time with the baby.

Starting in real estate

In 1990, DePaulo was ready to begin selling residential real estate.

She initially endeavoured to also work at Canada Trust, but soon found her demanding real estate work required her full-time attention.

DePaulo then left Canada Trust to devote herself exclusively to her real estate career.

In June of 1990, DePaulo joined the former Alec Murray Real Estate firm, then the largest independent real estate broker in Ontario, as a licensed real estate agent.

DePaulo also became a member of the Metropolitan Hamilton Real Estate Board and her sales area of metro Hamilton then, as now, tended to mainly cover West-Hamilton, Ancaster, Dundas, the West Mountain and Flamborough.

"When I was new to the business, I hosted open houses for established agents," DePaulo notes. "It was a good way for me to introduce myself to homebuyers. I advertised the open houses and passed out lots of business cards."

Determined efforts to succeed

But her determined efforts didn't end there.

"I also often called expired listings to see if the

vendors were interested in re-listing with someone new," she says.

"And I knocked on doors in neighbourhoods and asked the homeowners if they were interested in listing their homes or planned on getting into the real estate market in the near future. I needed to introduce myself – and my efforts seemed to be getting some results."

In 1991, after just one year of selling real estate, she was already getting recognized as a top sales representative, winning Silver honours for Alec Murray Real Estate. It was the first of many such distinctions.

Month after month, although the company had grown to more than 300 sales representatives, DePaulo's name was frequently listed among Alec Murray's top producers. Although a newcomer, DePaulo consistently ranked in the top 5 per cent.

Top Producer

In 1992, DePaulo was named Top Producer 1992 and won Gold recognition that same year – just her second year in real estate.

Alec Murray himself wrote numerous letters of congratulations and praise to DePaulo. But one letter, two years later, would signify the end of one era and the start of another.

Meanwhile, in 1993, DePaulo had to entirely give up her part-time work at Canada Trust – she'd already limited her involvement to Monday shifts only – to devote herself exclusively to arranging real estate sales only.

"I hated to give up the Canada Trust job," she recalls.

"I'd been in banking for so long, since 1975, that it was in my blood," she explains. "But I got so busy I had to give up the bank job. And by this point, I felt my future was in real estate."

Devoted to selling real estate

In September 1994, Murray wrote again thanking DePaulo for her "dedication, support and loyalty."

But Murray then went on to advise: "It is that time in one's life when changes are necessary." He then disclosed that he had decided to merge his company and chose Royal LePage "because of its new corporate structure, its direction and the fact that it is an all-Canadian company."

Although approached by competing real estate firms with offers to join their organizations, DePaulo decided to continue working in her same Ancaster office under the new Royal LePage banner.

And it didn't take her long to again make her presence felt, winning the Royal LePage President's Gold Award in 1994 – her first year with the newly merged real estate office.

This major award goes only to the top 10 per cent of Royal LePage sales representatives across Canada

The following year, she again won the President's Gold Award.

And, DePaulo was again named the top producer for her real estate office.

In 1996, DePaulo was again ranking with the top producers for sales, month after month after month.

And, she again won Top Producer for her real estate office for the year 1996.

Lifetime achievement award

In fact, starting in 1993 and for every year since, DePaulo has won the President's Gold Award.

DePaulo has also won the prestigious Royal LePage Director's Platinum Award, when it was introduced in 1998, and every year since.

She's also won the Royal LePage Award of Excellence: Lifetime Member, for 10 solid years of exemplary performance in the real estate industry.

As well, for her office, with the exception of 1993 and 1997, DePaulo has been Top Agent every one of the past 10 years straight, an absolutely remarkable achievement in a highly competitive field.

DePaulo has also consistently ranked among the top real estate agents throughout the Metropolitan Hamilton Real Estate Board.

Move to franchise operation

In the late 1990s, DePaulo's real estate office again went through a transition, this time to emerge as a franchise operation known as Royal LePage State Realty.

DePaulo is also very proud of being part of this company – "It's a really terrific company" – and the Royal LePage organization.

Now one of the largest real estate firms in Canada, it all started nearly 90 years ago with realtor Albert E. LePage, who revolutionized the Canadian real estate industry by becoming the first agent in Toronto to turn the buying and selling of homes into a professional enterprise.

Not only did LePage help found the Toronto Real Estate Board – which helped raise industry standards – he routinely took buyers house to house by car, followed up on inquiries and placed many descriptive advertisements in newspapers – all industry standards today.

Words to live by

LePage firmly believed the real estate industry should exhibit principled conduct and the highest ethical and moral standards.

These ideals were maintained when the A. E. LePage real estate firm merged with Royal Trust in 1984 to form Royal LePage.

And those ideals are very much embraced by DePaulo, who states: "When Albert E. LePage started up the Toronto Real Estate Board, his vision was to present impeccable professionalism, principled conduct and the highest moral and ethical standards. Today, almost 90 years later, these same principles still guide me in everything I do."

DePaulo finds being part of Royal LePage has many advantages, including being associated with a familiar and trusted name in real estate, national advertising campaigns and a national residential referral network.

Website advantage

Another very big benefit is the award-winning

www.royallepage.ca website, which receives well over a 100-million hits monthly.

The website also features continuously updated photo-listings for over 30,000 properties across Canada, survey data, maps, feature sheets and first-time buyers' section with mortgage calculator, descriptive community search information with postal codes and e-mail links to listing agents.

DePaulo makes regular use of the website in addition to advertising her clients' homes in various print media.

It's a winning combination that provides great exposure for her client's homes.

As well, if a client is moving outside of Ontario, DePaulo can tap into the very extensive relocation services network offered by Royal LePage, which has relocation service arrangements with over 600 companies and routinely relocates well in excess of 5,000 people every year.

Part of a big organization

Royal LePage is hands down the largest Canadian, publicly owned national full-service real estate brokerage business in the nation, with more than 8,400 sales representatives, coast to coast. Of these, 4,500 are in the province of Ontario.

Residential sales account for 80 per cent of the business of Royal LePage, which has 450 locations, of which 197 are in Ontario.

Royal LePage offers property appraisals through its professional services division and the company also has a commercial real estate division and a property management division controlling over 53 million square feet of space.

The company name is well known to consumers and to industry professionals who regularly turn to such Royal LePage publications as The Survey of Canadian House Prices and the Annual Market Survey when it comes to identifying and analyzing real estate market trends.

Royal LePage and DePaulo are also proud supporters of Smiles program that benefits The Children's Hospital at the Hamilton Health Sciences Corporation (Chedoke/McMaster hospitals).

Bringing 'Smiles' to children

"Each time I list or sell a 'Smiles' home, I earmark a portion of my receipts from that sale to be contributed the 'Smiles' fund," DePaulo explains.

Her contributions and those of other participating Royal LePage agents are contributed to the 'Smiles' fund and officially presented each May during the televised Children's Hospital Mother's Day Telethon.

As well, every time DePaulo lists or sells a home, she also donates a portion of her commission to the Women's Shelter Foundation.

Her donations, and the contributions of other Royal LePage agents are accumulated and periodically forwarded to Hamilton area women's shelters.

DePaulo has also been active in the Ancaster community: contributing her time and assistance and financial support to St. Joachim and other schools; sponsoring, in the past, youth soccer and hockey; supporting hospital fund-raising campaigns and generally helping the community any way she can think of.

Giving back

"I think it's important to give something back to your community, whether it's a donation of time or money," she says. "The main thing is to make a contribution towards making the community a better place."

DePaulo likes the sense of freedom that comes with being a real estate sales representative.

"I like being my own boss, not being chained to a desk and punching a clock," she says.

"And I can set my own hours – so instead of working 9 am to 5 pm, I'll work 9 am to midnight, weekends included," she adds with a laugh.

Flexible hours

Still, DePaulo is pleased her flexible hours have allowed her to attend school plays and sports events. She's also been able to help out as the treasurer of her children's school. And she enjoys spending quiet time at home.

"When I'm not crazy-busy, I like spending time at home, cooking meals, going for walks – and I love gardening, not that I often have time to do any," she says wistfully.

But DePaulo is also quick to point out that whatever work freedom she does enjoy is owed in part to her husband's assistance.

"My husband also has a real estate license, he's been working as my office assistant and he's recently decided to get more actively involved in real estate," DePaulo notes.

"I'm out so much with clients that I really depend on my husband to keep our household running smoothly," she acknowledges.

"I couldn't work the hours I do without his support as I'm rarely at home when I'm busy."

Depends on husband

DePaulo says that with her husband's help on the home front, she's can focus on real estate.

"I really thrive on my job," she says, noting that success in real estate depends on mastering several key elements.

"You have to be extremely well organized and flexible so you can set and change clients' appointments to suit them," she notes.

"You also have to make sure the computer technology you're using is completely up to date so you can quickly access listings information and data and keep current with the market," she adds.

People skills vital

"But I think the most important thing is people skills," DePaulo asserts.

"You need to be able to really listen to your clients and understand their needs and have a lot of empathy for their concerns," she says, noting that her psychology background has likely helped.

"Sometimes you're dealing with divorce situations or people who have financial concerns or are under a lot of stress, so it's important to be compassionate and understanding," she adds.

"Your clients should be able to put their trust and confidence in you to do a good job and treat whatever personal information you become privy to in a confidential manner."

Yet as demanding as this role can be, DePaulo wouldn't trade it for anything.

"I love my job – it's terrific," DePaulo says enthusiastically, "because I get to assist people in buying a home, in making the biggest financial commitment of their lives."

"And it's very satisfying being able to help people to realize their dreams."

Sue DePaulo's tips for success:

1. Always put your client's interests ahead of your own. Make the client your top priority.
2. Live and work by the Golden Rule: Treat others, as you'd like to be treated yourself.
3. Make time to give back to your community whether in time or cash contributions.
4. Follow a code of conduct that is ethical, moral and principled.
5. Always strive to be the best you can be and with each achievement set the bar higher.
6. Don't be afraid to try something new: Great real estate agents can start out as bankers.
7. Promptly return phone calls and spend as much time as necessary meeting your clients' needs.
8. Listen to your clients. Understand what they're saying and address their concerns.
9. Treat your clients well and build your business on referrals and repeat business.
10. Don't just satisfy your clients; delight them by going the extra mile to find the deal that's best for them.

Ken Lindsay

Chapter Six

Ken Lindsay

Home Ownership Help at Mortgage Financial

"It comes down to the volume of business we do. It's buying power... We can benefit the customer, whether they're well-off or have financial concerns by shopping the market on their behalf to get the best mortgage possible for them at the best terms and rates,"

- Ken Lindsay

At a Glance: Ken Lindsay and Mortgage Financial:

Ken Lindsay
Age: 39
Title: President, Mortgage Financial Corporation.

Claim to fame: Lindsay heads highly successful mortgage broker firm and shops the market to find the best possible mortgages for clients. He puts together mortgages that best meet a client's needs. His firm has grown steadily over the years and now provides employment for several brokers plus support staff. It's now one of the largest independent mortgage brokers in south-western Ontario.

Financial Data: Largely undisclosed. However, this is a multi-million-dollar company, growing at an average rate of 30 per cent growth per year.

Personal: Resides in Ancaster with wife Monika. The couple have 3 sons: Max, 7, and four-year-old twins Brad and Jeff.

For More information:
Contact: Mortgage Financial Corporation:
(905) 529-2521. Toll Free Line: 1-866-604-8860.
Fax: (905) 525-9701.
Address: 12 Ray St. South, Hamilton, Ont. L8P 3V2.

Chapter Six

Ken Lindsay

Home Ownership Help
at Mortgage Financial

For too many people, the dream of home ownership remains nothing more than a dream.

Ken Lindsay makes that dream a reality.

Lindsay, 39, is a mortgage broker: He shops the market for the best mortgage deals he can find his clients – even those with poor credit ratings.

"We take pride in generating savings to the customer," notes Lindsay, president of Mortgage Financial Corporation.

"Whether the client is financially successful or is currently facing financial issues, we can save them some money by shopping the mortgage market to find a deal that best meets their needs," he explains in an interview at company headquarters on Ray Street South, Hamilton.

"There aren't too many people who can go to a bank on their own and get a better deal than we can, generally," Lindsay asserts.

Buying power

"That's because we're also able to exercise a fair amount of buying power, some real financial clout, given the amount of business we bring to the banks," adds Lindsay, very much a hands-on broker who continues to personally arrange mortgages on behalf of his many clients.

"And for those customers who have been turned down by a bank, we're often able to get them a mortgage – sometimes from the same bank that turned them down – by negotiating a deal that works for everyone."

Financial lenders, including banks and trust companies, pay the firm a finder's fee/commission for bringing them ready-to-go mortgage deals involving financially secure borrowers.

A win-win situation

The arrangement also works well for banks, which rely on the broker to bring them mortgage business.

As well, the bank gets to sit back while the broker does the bulk of the work. And the bank will withhold any commission until the successful completion of a mortgage deal.

"It's basically a risk-free undertaking for the banks – it's really good for all of the financial institutions," Lindsay notes, "and the banks remain suppliers of the mortgage funds in most cases."

And for would-be homeowners who have credit difficulties and have been turned down by the banks, there is still hope.

Mortgage help for everyone

Mortgage Financial charges a fee to these less-secure clients to arrange a mortgage on their behalf, normally at somewhat higher interest rates to reflect the added degree of risk involved.

"Usually we can negotiate a deal at virtually no cost to the mortgage-borrower – they literally have nothing to lose and everything to gain with lower rates and better terms," Lindsay says.

He notes these clients account for about 75 per cent of his business, "and we can sometimes even beat the rates the banks offer their own staff."

"Even for the clients who are not financially secure, we can often put together a deal that's not a whole lot more expensive than what someone in a more financially advantageous position would be taking on," Lindsay adds.

"It comes down to the volume of business we do – it's buying power," the amiable broker explains.

Even a modest difference in interest rates can prove substantial.

For example, before factoring in property

taxes, a $100,000 mortgage, amortized over 20 years (the full lifespan of the mortgage) at a 3 per cent interest rate would cost the borrower $554 in monthly principal-and-interest payments.

The same mortgage with a 4 percent interest rate would push the monthly payments to more than $600 and a 5 per cent increases the payment needed to nearly $660.

Small rate change: big difference

A further increase of less than one per cent – to 5.75 per cent – inflates the monthly payments to still more costly $700.

Quite clearly, even a small difference in mortgage interest rates can have a very significant impact on payment levels and affordability.

Lindsay and Mortgage Financial broker-agents routinely save their clients many thousands of dollars in mortgage payments annually by arranging lower-rate mortgages.

"We can benefit the customer, whether they're well-off or have financial concerns by shopping the market on their behalf to get the best mortgage possible for them at the best terms and rates," Lindsay asserts.

"If they're financially well-off, we can get them better rates and better terms than they'll likely be able to get on their own," he states.

"And, if the client is struggling a little or working through some financial issues, we can, in most cases, get them a pretty good mortgage when they otherwise might not be able to get any mortgage at all," he adds.

Lindsay's Mortgage Financial firm is today one of the largest independent mortgage brokers in south-western Ontario, with business volume in the tens of millions of dollars.

Success story built on determination

How he rose to become a leading mortgage broker and highly successful businessman is a story that begins in the city of Brantford.

Sometimes called the Telephone City, Brantford is famous as the home of Alexander Graham Bell, the late, great inventor of the world's most-used communications device.

Brantford is also renowned as the birthplace of Wayne Gretzky, arguably the greatest hockey player who has ever lived.

The city, which is also the birthplace of the late, great comic actor Phil Hartman, has a leafy charm that extends well beyond the banks of Grand River that runs through it.

But Brantford is also well known for hard times and failed industries. Numerous industries have vacated the city and others have simply closed. In the midst of economic devastation, too many local citizens adopted a "no you can't" attitude toward success.

Yet, it was in this oft-times negative civic atmosphere and outlook that a young Ken Lindsay's entrepreneurial spirit would emerge.

Driven by desire to Achieve

"I think I've always wanted to succeed in a business of some kind," Lindsay recalls.

Driven by a desire to achieve, Lindsay left Brantford for Hamilton in 1982 where he attended McMaster University and completed a Bachelor of Economics (B.Econ) degree in 1986.

After graduating, he began working as a salesman in Toronto for the 3M company, selling business equipment, including fax machines to corporate customers.

"Fax machines were brand new to the market back then," he recalls with a smile, "and I can remember having to convince many CEOs to fax instead of courier information to their clients."

But convince them he did, rising quickly to become one the company's most successful salesmen in Ontario.

He was also earning $47,000 a year at a time when $30,000 was considered a substantial middle-class income.

Discovering the value of real estate

During his first year out of university, Lindsay invested some of his 3M salesman earnings into the purchase both halves of a two-family, semi-detached duplex house in Hamilton's leafy Westdale community – the home of McMaster University - which he then rented out as student housing.

The experience of buying up real estate provided Lindsay with some personal experience of what it means to obtain and maintain mortgages.

It also taught him location and timing are everything.

"Not only had I bought two houses ideally

located right near the university, I also bought just before the real estate boom," he recalls, noting he bought the duplex for $110,000 in 1987 and sold just two years later for $220,000 – twice what he'd originally paid.

Huge return on investment

The huge return on investment would later be used, in part, to buy his own home and as seed money to fund the start-up of his own company.

The income from the student rental housing also boosted his already substantial income from 3M, a sales job that pushed Lindsay to find the most effective marketing methods around to sell relatively unknown fax machine products.

"It was an opportunity – and a challenge," he recalls with a grin.

"Fax machines were a new concept and they were expensive," he adds.

"The cheapest model was $6,000 – and the actual machine was no bigger than the ones out today, but it was in a big case to justify the price."

A fateful foray into mortgage brokering

After three years with 3M, Lindsay was ready to take on another challenging opportunity.

He found that opportunity in Oakville – and it marked his first, fateful foray into the world of mortgage brokering.

In 1989, he began working as a mortgage broker for Goldmore Financial (now known as The

Mortgage Department), an Oakville-based mortgage broker.

That same year, he decided to set down some roots, and he bought a house in Burlington.

Lindsay soon discovered that although he was working for a mortgage broker in Oakville, "most of my clients were in Hamilton, so I was also being drawn to this city."

"I really like Hamilton," Lindsay asserts.

"It's smaller than Toronto but it still has everything a big city has to offer, and the people are very friendly," he notes.

"I also found the lenders here in Hamilton to be quite approachable. This is a blue-collar town but approaching the size of a metropolis."

Lindsay decided to lay down more Steel City roots, actively seeking out local lenders while also building the bulk of his clientele base in Hamilton.

Winning combination in Hamilton

"I found the winning combination in Hamilton," he explains.

"Hamilton offers a good source of approachable private lenders and a sizeable client base of people who need mortgages and don't hesitate to turn to us for service and advice."

The transition from broker to broker-owner took place incrementally, over the course of a few years, during which time Lindsay built a solid reputation as a straight-forward broker who worked closely with clients to achieve the best mortgages possible on their behalf.

His growing success was also forged on his willingness to listen closely to what client's were saying, concerning both their need for a mortgage and their income and affordability concerns. His approach inevitably resulted in the creation of custom-made mortgages and very satisfied clients.

And his approach succeeded in attracting a seemingly never-ending series of referrals that continues to this day.

In fact, his company owes much of its continued prosperity to referrals based on exemplary past performance.

The dawn of Mortgage Financial

In 1991, Lindsay took the plunge and founded his own company on King Street West in Hamilton, near Queen Street.

And starting up Mortgage Financial in Canada's Steel City was not without risk.

"It's always a major adjustment to go from something that's relatively secure to something that's new and different," Lindsay recalls.

"But I knew this was something I wanted to do, something I really had to do and I was prepared to take on the risks of venturing out on my own."

Although Toronto was then, as now, the main financial centre of Ontario and Canada, Lindsay saw in Hamilton a vibrant city rich in potential.

"With Hamilton, I saw a service-oriented opportunity," he recalls, "and I got into this business when it was relatively young so I could build on my modest investment in my company."

"In Canada, brokers are involved in only about 22 per cent of all mortgages, while in the United States, the level is 78 per cent – so there's a lot of growth potential for the mortgage brokering business in this country," he adds.

"Back in 1991, my company was very small," he recalls. "It was just myself and one other broker – but we were ready to grow from there."

Lindsay would come to outgrow that first location and he moved, in 1998, to his current headquarters on Ray Street, just a few blocks away from the original offices.

He owns the stately office building on Ray Street South – purchased for $171,000 – that was converted from a 130-year-old mansion a short walk from the Scottish Rite.

Risk level increased to spur growth

"That year, 1998, was really a very tough year," Lindsay recalls, shaking his head.

"I owed $50,000 in taxes at that point, plus I had just put $50,000 down on the Ray Street building and had a mortgage for the rest," he adds.

"My wife had just had twins and we bought a van. Altogether, it was a larger debt-load than I'd ever experienced and I had to work many long, hard hours to generate sufficient income to keep it all under control."

Weathering that financial situation gave the young mortgage broker some first-hand sympathy for what many people encounter when they take on the heady costs associated with a mortgage, other debts and, of course, the never-ending costs of raising a family.

Simply put, Lindsay also came to appreciate, in 1998, what it means to be stretched to max.

"That was the most risk I've ever taken on in my life," he acknowledges with raised eyebrows.

"But it motivated me to succeed," he adds.

"I know what our clients go through. I've been there. I know what it's like to wonder if you'll qualify for a mortgage and what it's like to have to make those payments."

The experience would also have a profound affect on Lindsay.

"To stay on top of it all, I consolidated all my debts into a better package and started working away at paying it down," he explains.

"But it was necessary at that time to take on this debt and the business had to rank high on the priority list. It had to be done – so I did it."

Pay-as-you-go approach

"I now pay as I go, all the time, as much as humanly possible," Lindsay asserts.

"And I try to take on very little debt. In fact, I make a real effort to keep my fixed costs and debt to a minimum."

There's also no question his own experience with grappling with personal mortgages and debt helped make Lindsay a better, more effective, understanding mortgage broker.

Inside his expansive Ray Street building with ornate woodwork and high-ceilings, Lindsay can often be found on the phone or plying the computer at his oft-cluttered desk (yet he can somehow manage to find any desired document on that same messy desk surface).

In running Mortgage Financial, he's assisted by his brother Mike Lindsay and a dedicated support staff. Also helping drive Mortgage Financial to new heights is a team of broker-agents.

Team effort

"I really like our office atmosphere," Lindsay acknowledges with a grin.

"They're a great group and we enjoy bouncing ideas off each other. It's impressive when I think that we have a large group of people all helping each other out."

While he still handles some deals directly, Lindsay is also heavily involved in running his office, handling payroll and provide problem-solving and direction skills to the company.

"To a certain extent, I depend on my broker-agents to build business volume," he explains.

"But I also still enjoy arranging mortgages myself whenever the opportunity presents itself," Lindsay adds.

"Having the Kronas Group – one of the largest private lenders in the Hamilton area – right in our building is also a big benefit," he notes.

"Getting financing for a mortgage is often as simple as going upstairs in this building for a visit with someone from the Kronas Group."

Soon after Mortgage Financial's founding in 1991, the young company began achieving some impressive profit growth.

That trend has carried on, and the company's

profits have continued to average 30 per cent growth over the past few years.

The company now arranges more than $100-million worth of mortgages annually and grosses in excess of $2-million in annual revenue.

Much of the fast growing profit – figures are confidential – is reinvested in the company and in the financing of mortgages.

Impressive growth

"Our profit growth has really exceeded all expectations," Lindsay says, noting Mortgage Financial is now one of the largest independent mortgage broker firms in the whole of south-western Ontario.

The company has 28 broker-agents and support staff in Hamilton, plus another three broker-agents at a branch office in Brantford.

The year 1991 also marked another very important milestone: The same year Lindsay started up his company, he also married his girlfriend Monica.

His wife, also now 39, bought their family home in 1990 for $130,000 and the happy couple took residence there on marrying the following year.

They rented in out a basement apartment for the next six years until the house was sold in 1997 for $165,000. His wife is also no slouch on the business front – she's a full partner in the highly successful Fast Eddies drive-through fast food chain of restaurants.

The couple now reside with their three children: Max 7, and four-year-old twins Brad and Jeff, in the Meadowlands neighbourhood in Hamilton's Ancaster community.

Lindsay believes much of his firm's success is owed to its prominence in the Hamilton market and its ability to arrange an array of mortgages.

"Our business volume helps us achieve good placement of mortgages at more than competitive rates," he notes, "and I think that, more than anything else, has helped us to grow, year by year. I anticipate growth continuing in the 30 per cent range, but I'd be happy with even half of that."

And Lindsay still clearly enjoys his hands-on approach to brokering mortgages.

"We do all the negotiating and shopping around for rates on the client's behalf," he says, adding "in most cases, most of shopping is done in my head because I know which lenders to use and where to place a given mortgage."

The shopping is also done before meeting with clients. By the time an actual meeting between customer and broker takes place, The Mortgage Financial representative usually has in place a short list of advantageous mortgage options for the client to choose from.

Clients also benefit from Lindsay's access to a large pool of lenders, the negotiating clout his volume of business gives him with the banks and his industry savvy and his ability to negotiate a win-win deal for the customer and lender.

Tailor-made mortgages

"We can custom tailor a mortgage to the customer's needs right off the bat because we have so many lenders and mortgage products to choose from," he notes.

To tailor a mortgage to the client's needs,

Lindsay or one of his broker-agents will sit down with the customer and determine what their income levels are, how much mortgage they can afford to carry, what payment schedules are best-suited for them, how determined they are to pay off the mortgage and what other options are preferred.

Mortgage options can include the length of amortization – whether the total mortgage life span runs 10, 15, 20 or 25 years.

A shorter amortization means the mortgage is paid off entirely much more quickly, but the weekly or monthly payments are much higher than they would be with a longer amortization period.

Regardless of the amortization period, weekly payments (also payments every two weeks) are often recommended as they effectively translate into an extra monthly payment each year, which in turn means the mortgage is being reduced a little more quickly and conveniently.

Many mortgage options to choose from

Mortgage options can include a number of variations in the length of the term – whether one wants to go six months, one year, two years, three years or five years before renewing the mortgage.

The borrower may also want to knock down the size of the mortgage by having extra payment privileges that allow for larger payments or a lump sum payment or both during the mortgage term.

A down payment of 25 per cent or more of the purchase price will not only dramatically reduce the size of the resulting mortgage, it will also save the borrower costs of getting the mortgage insured by Canada Mortgage and Housing Corporation. CMHC insurance – for high leverage loans of more than 75 per cent of the purchase price – often adds several thousand dollars to the size of the mortgage.

There are still also mortgage variations, including fixed rates that lock you in at a set interest rate for the mortgage term, and variable rates, which are tied to market interest rates and follow those rates up or down.

Variable rates are often considered attractive to borrowers if they anticipate rates remaining low or falling. But if rates rise, the borrower pays the higher rate.

Fixed rates are sometimes a little more costly, but they provide the stability of certainty over the level of interest rate the borrower will pay.

Lindsay notes his ability to draw on a number of lenders means he can offer just about any mortgage package combination imaginable.

"If you, as an individual, are still limiting yourself to one lending institution, you pretty much have to take what you can get – and that's often not the greatest deal that's out there in the marketplace," he observes.

Sense of satisfaction

Lindsay also derives a considerable sense of satisfaction in helping clients obtain the mortgage that's best for them.

"It's a great feeling when we're able to get someone a terrific interest rate and terms," he says.

"And it's also a great feeling when someone

who figured they'd never be able to buy a house is able to get a mortgage through us and achieve the dream of home ownership," he adds.

Despite the obvious merit of using a broker's services, the mortgage broker industry hasn't always had a sterling reputation.

As recently as the early 1970s, brokers were viewed with a disdain normally reserved for used car salesmen.

That image, never really accurate, was also seriously outdated, going back to an era in which there was little regulation of the mortgage broker industry and greater potential for abuse.

The industry is today governed by the Ontario Ministry of Consumer and Financial Services and there are clear-cut rules and regulations for fair conduct.

Unfortunately, old, tired and largely unfair impressions can sometimes linger on.

Until recent decades, mortgage brokers were seen as lenders of last resort, unsavoury people who arranged loans, at punitive interest rates, for equally unsavoury clients or for hapless victims who couldn't afford to take on any mortgage or loan.

Such victims then found their high-interest mortgages to be crushing debt loads.

Improving image

That unseemly image of the mortgage broker was rarely deserved and largely inaccurate, except for the enduring role as a lender of last resort: Mortgage brokers have, in fact, traditionally been just that: lenders of last resort, the last people you can turn to when the financial institutions have turned you down.

And that role – a heroic role in the eyes of many borrowers – has continued to some degree right up to the present.

Heroic role continues

"A good 25 per cent of our business comes from people who have been turned down by their bank for a mortgage," Lindsay notes, "with the other 75 per cent consisting mainly of people who have no difficulty getting a mortgage – they just want to use our broker services so we can shop the market to get them better rates."

"But it was actually the reverse back when I started in this business," he adds.

"The vast majority of people using broker services back then had been turned down by the banks and were using us as a lender of last resort. And that was only ten years ago."

Despite the trend to lower-risk lending, Lindsay makes it clear he'd "never want to give up that 25 per cent of higher risk lending, because it's a good source of business and a great way to help people out."

"In fact, we sometimes have some higher-risk borrowers coming directly to us, without even going to a bank first, because they don't feel comfortable dealing with a bank and they fear being rejected when they apply for a mortgage," he elaborates.

"We're happy to deal with low-risk and high-risk borrowers."

And today's uncertain times, there are growing numbers of people facing severe financial difficulties for the first time, he points out.

"Not only is the old life-long jobs era long over, we've seen a lot of corporate downsizing and elimination of jobs," Lindsay notes.

"Today, more people than not have credit problems, and we do what we can to help," he adds.

Turning to mortgage brokers for help

"We'll even help people get credit cards and re-establish their credit ratings and, of course, get them a good mortgage," Lindsay explains.

"We're in the business of giving a lot of people an opportunity they didn't think even existed – and they're not in way overpaying for that opportunity."

Lindsay notes greater numbers of people are turning to mortgage brokers – and he expects that trend to continue.

"More and more people are gradually coming around to the idea of using a mortgage broker to do all the work for you – for free in most cases – to arrange your mortgage," he observes.

Brokering better deals

"After all, people think nothing of using an insurance broker to get the best insurance deal, and it's becoming that way with using mortgage brokers to get the best mortgage deals," he adds.

In fact, it's difficult to understand why anyone would not want to use the services of a reputable mortgage broker.

"We'll often do 100-plus mortgages a month,

whereas most people will do perhaps one or two in their lifetime – so how can they compete with us for the best deal? We know which lenders to go to which deals can be improved, all of the ins and outs of mortgages – it's what we do."

And the benefits of using a broker go beyond the financial.

"We'll get you the same or lower rate than the bank is offering – usually a lower rate," Lindsay asserts.

"And we'll get the job done more quickly and efficiently with less aggravation for the borrower to deal with," he notes.

"We can also provide substantially more choice in mortgage products and terms," he adds.

"More people are finding they'd much rather leave the task of arranging a mortgage to an expert, a mortgage broker, who can do all the work for them to get the deal that's best for them."

Ken Lindsay's tips for success:

1. Use debt as a tool to achieve the wealth that equity brings. Recognize that debt to gain an appreciating asset – such as a mortgage to buy a house – is good debt that helps builds equity.
2. Build equity as this means building wealth. Why pay rent to a landlord when you can take on a mortgage and ownership of your own home – and your own destiny.
3. Consider renting out part of you home so that tenants pay your mortgage for you.
4. Control debt – don't let debt control you. Even good debt can be too much of a good thing. It's important to reduce debts.
5. Think about what you want to achieve and set about making your dreams a reality.
6. If you'd like to start a business, first get experience and education in that field.
7. Do market research. Take a methodical, thorough approach to building the business.
8. Be prepared to work long and hard to earn a measure of success in your endeavour.
9. Don't be afraid to take on debt – and risk – to finance the achievement of your dreams.
10. Any risk you take on should be a calculated risk. You should be confident of success.

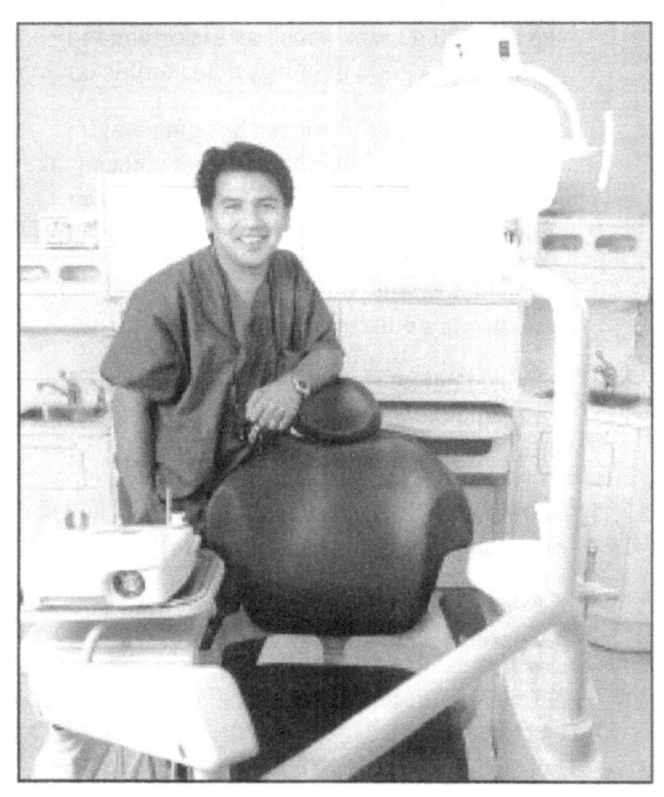

Dr. Roland Estrabillo

Chapter Seven

Dr. Roland Estrabillo

On the leading edge of dentistry

"Success is never something you achieve all by yourself. It's when learn from others and share your own experiences that you improve in the process. And everyone benefits from this type of sharing."

- Dr. Roland Estrabillo

At a Glance: Dr. Roland Estrabillo:

Dr. Roland Estrabillo
Age: 42
Title: Dentist.

Claim to fame: He takes an innovative approach to his dentistry practice, employing the latest technological advancements to make dental procedures as fast, efficient and comfortable as possible. He's also a lifelong student who continues to learn from his mentors: fellow dentists, staff and friends from all walks of life who have helped him overcome problems and achieve new levels of success in his demanding career.

Financial Data: Largely undisclosed. However, this is a multi-million-dollar practice, growing steadily.

Personal: Resides in Dundas with wife Maria. The couple have four children: sons Jean, 13; Sam, 9; and Nathan, 7; and daughter Andrea, 3.

For More information:
Contact: Dr. Roland Estrabillo: (905) 387-2600
Fax: (905) 387-2617
Address: Hamilton location: 860 Upper Wentworth Street, Hamilton, Ontario, L9A 4W4.
Address: Ancaster location: 201 Wilson Street, Ancaster, Ontario.
email: drestrabillo@mountaincable.net

Chapter Seven

Dr. Roland Estrabillo
On the leading edge of dentistry

With a growing dental practice and booming consulting business, you might expect to find Dr. Roland Estrabillo spending his spare time on the greens.

Instead, we find him on the couch – cradling his three-year-old daughter Andrea in his arms.

The happy domestic scene takes place at his Dundas home – which happens to back onto the Dundas Valley Golf and Country Club.

But while the links are just steps away, they might as well be worlds away for this dedicated dad of four young children.

Estrabillo has spent the past two years "being Mr. Mom," while his wife Maria, a 37-year-old dental lab technician, completes a degree in dentistry from a Manila Central University back in the Philippines, with an additional two years of qualifying studies back in Canada to follow.

"I love this – it's wonderful getting the opportunity to spend this much time with my children, it's a great experience" Estrabillo grins as his daughter cuddles closer.

"I'm really learning a lot – especially about all the work my wife did all the time that I just took for granted," he adds in an interview at the big two-storey, 4,000-square-foot, four-bedroom, eat-in kitchen, Dundas home he bought four years ago.

A grateful Mr. Mom

"It's great being Mr. Mom," he grins.

"But it's a lot of hard work and I'm really starting to appreciate a lot more all the things my wife took care of – feeding and clothing the kids, laundry, helping with homework – without ever saying a word about it," he adds.

"This has taught us all a good lesson, that we should do more to help out with the many household chores."

Estrabillo says he misses his wife but wanted her to have the opportunity to further her career in dentistry beyond the dental laboratory she's operated for many years.

"My wife is very important to me and getting along without her here at home can be a real challenge," he admits.

"But we all go through challenges in life and they make us stronger and help us to see things differently," he adds.

"Life is an exciting learning experience. Right now I'm experiencing what it's like to spend more time with my children and it's wonderful. So often, we're distracted with other things and we overlook the good things in life."

Although it's a Saturday, Estrabillo has been up since 5 am, making croissants for the whole family, plus: ham, cheese and rice for nine-year-old Sam; bacon and eggs and a milkshake for 13-year-old son Jean, who assists in preparing this meal; marinated pork for seven-year-old Nathan and scrambled eggs and rice for Andrea.

The "Mr. Mom" role is just another facet of this dynamo dentist who recently opened a second Hamilton dental location – a major expansion in Hamilton's Ancaster community – and is also busily building a successful consulting business.

Born in the Philippines

Estrabillo's hard-driving success story begins half a world away in the rice paddies of the Philippines.

Roland Estrabillo was born Dec. 17, 1960, the youngest of eight children born to Engracio and Virginia Estrabillo.

It was, and remains, a close-knit family that prides itself on the success achieved by all family members.

From an early age, the young Estrabillo helped doing chores at his father's rice paddies and sugar cane fields on a farm on the outskirts of the little town of Magliman, with a population 1,000 farming souls.

"Growing up working class, we didn't have very much," Estrabillo recollects.

"But my dad was very ambitious and we all worked together, as expected, to do the best we could possibly do in the Philippines class system."

Father worked three jobs

In addition to farming, Estrabillo's hard-driving, entrepreneurial father ran his own trucking business and worked as a labourer at the Clark Air Force Base, the sprawling U.S. military base on the outskirts of the nearby community of San Fernando (population 50,000).

"My dad was very hard-working but he felt he was being passed over for promotions because he only had a Grade 2 education," Estrabillo recalls.

"He wanted a better life for us, so my dad did everything in his power to make sure all of his children had a good education," he adds.

"Dad saved up as much money as he could and he began sending us to university, one after the other."

Many Helping Hands

Estrabillo says that each child became university-educated in progression of age; they were expected to contribute to the financing of education for siblings following them.

"I guess the one advantage to my being the youngest is that I didn't have to sponsor anyone after me, I really only had to consider my own education," Estrabillo says with a chuckle.

After graduating from high school in San Fernando, Estrabillo studied preparatory medicine and medical technology at Far Eastern University in Manila from 1977 to 1980.

Canada bound

It was then that Estrabillo was ready to begin a familiar family migration to Canada. His sister Flora, now 65, had been the first in the family to emigrate to North America, settling first in Chicago and then moving to Hamilton to take a nursing position.

Eventually, the entire family would follow, including the parents who live in Hamilton but spend winters in the Philippines.

"My sister really started it all," Estrabillo notes. "She came to Hamilton because of greener pastures, greater opportunities. She's the reason we're all here."

A teenager arrives

A teenaged Estrabillo arrived in Canada from the Philippines in 1980.

He was 19 and his arrival in The True North, Strong and Free, was the realization of a long-held dream.

"When I got here I just breathed in the air and looked around me and I knew anything was possible – I knew nothing could stop me from accomplishing anything I set out to do," he recollects.

"Every Canadian has the opportunity to pursue anything they want to do. We are so truly fortunate here, it's unbelievable. It really is the land of opportunity."

Pursuing a career in medicine

On arrival, it was found that he was lacking calculus, so he redid Grade 13 at St. Thomas Moore and then enrolled at the University of Toronto where he studied natural sciences for the next two years while pursuing a career in medicine.

Estrabillo continued to pursue his medical studies, working summers and earning scholarships.

He was then ready for the next fateful step.

Estrabillo decide he would apply to the faculties of both medicine and dentistry – and he was accepted for both!

Doctor or dentist?

He turned to a friend, a professor in the faculty of nuclear medicine, who promptly asked the young man if he ever wanted to have a family and lead a normal life.

"I said yes," Estrabillo recalls, "and he told me to be a dentist, not a doctor, because doctors were always on call and had little family time or the time to lead a normal life."

Estrabillo took one year of dentistry studies and still wasn't convinced.

So he took another "and I knew then that I'd found what I was looking for."

"I'm very grateful for having been steering in this direction and even my own children are very interested in following me and becoming dentists when they grow up. They've seen what dentistry is all about and they know it's a very worthwhile profession."

Setting up in Hamilton

After Estrabillo graduated in 1987 from the University of Toronto with a degree in dentistry, he returned to Hamilton that same year to set up practice on Upper Wentworth Street, in a little 1,500-square-foot location next to a supermarket in a strip mall opposite Lime Ridge Mall.

As the youthful dentist began building his fledgling practice, he displayed a voracious appetite for information and ideas, boldly seeking out new ways of doing things, new ways of approaching dentistry and life in general.

This openness to new ideas and to learning from the success of others would have a profound and last effect on him.

As Estrabillo continued to evolve as a successful dentist and explored all that life had to offer, a pivotal moment would occur in 1989 while he was enjoying the splendour of islands in the Pacific Ocean.

Swimming with the dolphins

The young dentist was wading into a warm water lagoon when a group of boisterous dolphins came splashing towards him, leaping through the water with unbridled joy.

As Dr. Roland Estrabillo stood transfixed in the water off a beach in Hawaii, the dolphins danced into the sheltered cove, chattering excitedly. They seemed to be beckoning the Hamilton dentist to join them.

"I had been looking in the water at brightly coloured fish when dolphins suddenly appeared," Estrabillo recalls in an interview at his Upper Wentworth Street offices.

Inspiring encounter

"They seemed so joyful, playful," he adds, "and I was fascinated by them."

Estrabillo threw caution to the winds and swam up to the dolphins.

"As I moved closer, they started swimming around me – they wanted to play," he recollects with a smile.

"I began following them, swimming with them, sometimes holding on to them and letting them pull me through the water – it was wonderful," he says.

"They have such a joyful attitude – wouldn't it be nice if you could be as happy as a dolphin in life," Estrabillo adds, "and I love their sense of freedom, confidence and happiness."

"It was an experience I'll never forget," he says of the happy encounter.

Inspired by the dolphins, Estrabillo placed likenesses of their happy images on his business cards and practice literature.

As well, he's decorated the walls of his Upper Wentworth Street office with large illustrations of dolphins at play.

He's also infused himself and his staff with a contagious dolphin-like, happy, confident attitude that puts patients at ease and makes trips to the dentist more enjoyable.

"I still love dolphins," Estrabillo admits in a recent interview at his home.

"The dolphin's image has become my own private signature – my patients are always bringing me little figurines and pictures of dolphins when they return from travelling. It's nice that people associate me with such a free and happy creature."

That Estrabillo would learn from dolphins and apply those lessons to his practice isn't surprising.

Estrabillo is determined to keep up in the rapidly evolving field of dentistry.

Lifelong learning

This dentist believes in lifelong learning and has long selected mentors from dentistry and other fields to give him guidance.

He attends many monthly seminars – including a 2002 seminar in Calgary that explored scientifically proven biologic alternative dentistry methods and procedures.

Estrabillo also mainly uses porcelain, limiting his use of metals to gold and titanium – and only for special applications where porcelain is not the most appropriate material to use. Porcelain is both durable and free of metals that might pose the risk of eventually leaching into the mouth.

And he invests in computer equipment; technology, methodologies and materials to ensure his busy practice can treat his many patients fast and efficiently.

For example, although he now regularly makes use of an anaesthesiologist, the I-V sedation certification he earned a few years ago means that he can, if need be, comfortably sedate his patients for longer periods while he performs cosmetic dentistry or full-mouth reconstructive surgery.

Growth through referrals

It's this constant attention to the needs and concerns of his patients that have helped this dentist's practice achieve remarkable ongoing growth through a steady stream of referrals.

Back in the early 1990s, while building his practice from scratch, Estrabillo outgrew his mall location within his first few years of running his dental practice.

And it was around that time, in 1991, that he'd just met a girl named Maria.

"We met by accident," Estrabillo recalls. "My cousin and her brother are friends and one they visited me in Hamilton and Maria was with them."

Estrabillo decided to have a second visit – and then bought an engagement ring and presented to her during a walk along Toronto's lakeshore.

"There was no question in my mind," he recalls. "She was my wife."

A few months later, the happy couple married in January 1992.

Later in 1992, Estrabillo moved his practice to renovated offices at his former home, just a little further north on Upper Wentworth Street.

But it wouldn't be long before he was again feeling cramped.

After expanding the number of operating rooms – known as operatories in the dental profession – to seven from four, he soon again found himself short of space.

Estrabillo begins to specialize

Although general family dentistry still accounted for 60 per cent of his practice in the mid-1990s, Dr. Estrabillo was concentrating more on full-mouth reconstructive dentistry as a growing, satisfying, part of his work.

And by the late 1990s, Estrabillo was even more heavily involved in personally performing the more complicated dental procedures and "more surgery and less drill-and-fill work," while his practice as a whole continued to perform general dentistry.

Teamwork

"We work as a team – for example, after the orthodontist and periodontist have treated the patient, I perform bridge work, teeth implants, crowns, veneers and cosmetic improvements to teeth," he explains.

"We've cut the time needed for a crown to half an hour from an hour, so the patient is more comfortable."

Dr. Estrabillo now takes two hours instead of seven to perform most full-mouth reconstruction procedures.

He notes this dentistry can improve chewing

efficiency, improve the functioning of the jaw, save teeth and "actually make people look younger with whiter, rearranged, straighter teeth which support the mouth better."

Opening a second location

By the late 1990s, Estrabillo also had an expanded patient load of more than 10,000 patients on file.

He then began contemplating moving to larger offices in Hamilton to serve his seemingly endlessly growing practice.

But instead of relocating, he expanded, keeping the Hamilton location while adding the Ancaster location featuring 20,000-square-feet of space and 10 operatories.

The Ancaster location will also house a dental lab for his wife Maria.

This will allow her to continue to provide dental lab technician work while working towards becoming a dentist.

She had been operating her own off-site laboratory for many years where she performed lab work for more complex crowns bridges and veneers.

Estrabillo's Ancaster location also features 64 parking spaces, separate offices for course work and a lecture hall that will seat 100 people.

The lecture hall will provide a venue for the consulting services, lectures and seminars his consulting firm provides to improve the care of teeth and expand public education in the field of dentistry.

As well, the lecture hall will allow Estrabillo to

share the knowledge he's learned, hosting regular seminars to impart product and methodology information to other dentists.

Sharing expertise

"We'd really like to share what we've learned here because everyone benefits when you can exchange ideas and consider new ways of doing things," Estrabillo explains, noting that the shared expertise should allow some fellow dentists to ramp up their practices and become more efficient providers of great dental care to their patients.

The services directed at fellow dentists will be provided through the separate consulting, training and lecturing company that Estrabillo has established.

"A few of my staff are involved and are on our lecture circuits," he notes.

Separate consulting firm

This separate firm allows Estrabillo and some of his staff to other dentists and their staff in the latest proven methodologies and procedures on a fee basis.

The two-storey Ancaster building, on Wilson between Jerseyville Road and Halson Avenue, had started construction in 2002, with completion expected in January 2003.

Both Hamilton locations are needed to keep pace with a burgeoning patient load that has now expanded to more than 12,000 patients on file.

Fuelling this impressive growth are referrals from satisfied patients who appreciate the extra care

Estrabillo takes to make visits pleasant and brief.

Numerous services offered

Also fuelling referrals are the many areas of expertise he can offer, including laser whitening, implant dentistry, alternative dentistry and bone scanning to reveal any bone-deep cavities or bone that has insufficient blood circulation.

Bone scans can also help diagnose hidden sources of chronic facial pain, increasing the likelihood of correction.

In fact, these various areas of expertise have drawn patients from coast to coast.

"A lot of people come to us for a whole range of services, including teeth implants – and we like to help them get their mouths back in great shape," Estrabillo smiles.

Exciting dentistry

Few people can combine the words 'dental' and 'exciting' in one sentence and make it work.

But Estrabillo is very convincing when he confides: "It's just so exciting to be able to provide all these dental services to our patients – and it's very gratifying when you can help so many people."

Estrabillo clearly loves dentistry, and he's always looking for new ways of expanding his knowledge and expertise in all matters dental.

He frequently works non-stop all day and into the evening, before heading home.

Estrabillo then makes dinner, takes care of

other household chores, and helps his children with their homework.

Then, from midnight to 2 am, it's his personal time when he reads about dentistry - "right now I'm studying head and neck pain in detail" – before going to bed to rise the next day at 5 am and do it all again.

Cutting back on sleep

Estrabillo greets my puzzled look with a grin. "That's right, I only sleep three hours a night – three to five hours is enough for me because I've trained myself to get by on very little sleep and still totally functional," explains the self-confessed workaholic, "and I think three hours is enough sleeping time."

"I do spend a lot time at work," he adds. "But I have a balanced life because I also devote a lot of time to my priorities. My highest priority is my spirituality – the Catholic religion, followed by our health, our family life and then my profession."

"The only thing I don't spend much time on is sleeping," he asserts. "But I feel fine, really good. I don't think I'm suffering from sleep deprivation."

Indeed, while others sleep, Estrabillo is active and enjoying a full life.

He estimates the wake-time he's gained by cutting back on his sleep will amount to a full 12 years over the course of his lifetime.

"Can you imagine what you can accomplish with 12 extra years?" he asks.

"I don't want to waste 12 years of my life on sleep," he adds.

"There isn't enough time in a day right now to

do all the things I want to do. But I can't give up sleep completely, so I get a few hours sleep and enjoy the extra time that I'm awake."

Learning from successful people

Estrabillo is clearly putting his added time to productive use: In addition to a thriving dental practice, keeping current with the latest dental techniques, lecturing on matters dental and devoting attention to his family, he continues to learn from other successful people,

"I'm still into mentoring," he confirms. "It's a good learning process to talk to people who have achieved success in their lives and learn from them."

And he's grateful for the input, advice and support he's received from his mentors, fellow dentists, staff and friends from all walks of life who have helped him overcome problems and achieve new levels of success in a demanding, time-consuming career.

"Success is never something you achieve all by yourself. It's when learn from others and share your own experiences that you improve in the process. And everyone benefits from this type of sharing."

Credits staff for success

Estrabillo directly attributes much of the success of his busy practice to his staff of 20 professionals, including four hygienists, three restorative hygienists (who can perform fillings work), support staff, and two dentist associates.

"My staff is great," he says with a grin.

"Without them I couldn't succeed. We do the best job we can - and we try to have fun in the process. We really enjoy our work."

He's also determined to make his office, himself and his entire staff as financially successful as possible.

In the past, as profits exceed target levels, the staff received a share of the surplus to spend or invest as they please.

More recently, he's replaced this profit-sharing plan with salary increases.

Keeping people motivated

"Money is a good motivator but after a while it doesn't have the same strong effect as an incentive," Estrabillo explains.

"So it's important to offer praise and to offer other motivations and opportunities to advance in their careers."

With that in mind, he's given some staff the opportunity to become shareholders in his training, lecturing and consulting company.

These staff will share in lecture fees in return for providing their services to the lecture circuit, the in-house lecture hall and at the seminars in the new building's offices.

"They're part of my team of total rehab experts," Estrabillo smiles.

Encouraging staff to pursue dreams

The Hamilton also provides his entire staff with the opportunity and ample encouragement to continue increasing their job qualifications and credentials.

"We want our staff to pursue their dreams, to go for higher education and take advantage of the opportunities they have to improve themselves and make this an even better practice," he explains.

As his practice continues to grow, Estrabillo sees further good times ahead for his entire staff.

"Every year we're experiencing phenomenal growth – the excitement level of the staff is just unbelievable," he exclaims.

"I see a very bright future for our staff, our patients, everyone involved. Life is a great learning experience – and we're always learning new ways to do what we do a little better."

Dr. Roland Estrabillo's tips for success:

1. Make successful people your mentors and learn from them.
2. Prioritize your life. Rank the things that are most important to your and devote the right amount of attention to each.
3. Don't be afraid to seek advice – or to give advice. You too have expertise to share.
4. Try to be all that you can be. It means hard work but the results are well worth it.
5. Don't deny yourself the simply pleasures of family life and spending quality time with loved ones.
6. Motivate your staff or supporters with praise and incentives to reward a good job.
7. Go the extra distance for clients (patients) and grow through steady referrals.
8. Make your client's (patient's) needs a top priority. Delight them and earned their repeat business.
9. Organize your time to achieve the most you can while still allowing relaxation time.
10. Find ways of taking yourself and endeavours to the next level. Build on your success, daily.

Teresa Cascioli

Chapter Eight

Lakeport Brewing

Pouring on the profits

"It really doesn't matter who you are. In this highly competitive industry, you still have to prove yourself. And I think we've done that by completely turning this company around."

- Teresa Cascioli

At a Glance: Teresa Cascioli and Lakeport Beverage Corp.

Teresa Cascioli
Age: 40
Title: President and Chief Executive Officer, Lakeport Beverage Corporation.
Claim to fame: She's a marketing genius who rescued Lakeport from bankruptcy and transformed it into a profitable entity and Ontario's fourth largest brewer. She's also the only woman to own and operate a major brewery in Canada.
Financial Data: Largely undisclosed. However, this is a multi-million-dollar company, growing steadily.
Personal: Single. Born and raised in Hamilton.
For More information:
Contact: Lakeport Beverage Corporation:
Phone: (905) 523-4200
Fax: (905) 523-6564.
Website: www.lakeportbeverage.ca
Address: 201 Burlington Street East, Hamilton, Ontario, L8L 4H2.

Chapter Eight

Lakeport Brewing

Pouring on the profits

Teresa Cascioli doesn't mind being called the 'Beer Babe' – she's too busy turning Lakeport Beverage Corp. into a huge success to take any offence.

Cascioli, single, and attractive, routinely shatters any image the heavily male-dominated brewing industry tries to pin on her.

When she took over Lakeport in November 1999, some in the industry's old boy's club were very quick to dismiss the leggy business executive as the 'Beer Babe', implying a more appropriate place for a buxom woman was in a sexist beer commercial, not at the helm of a serious business.

But Cascioli – the only female owner-operator of a major brewery in Canada – soon left her critics choking on their suds when she not only brought Lakeport out of bankruptcy, but quickly restored the Hamilton beer company to profitability.

"I really don't care what they call me," Cascioli, 40, asserts during an interview at Lakeport corporate headquarters, by the Lake Ontario shoreline in Hamilton.

"Frankly, gender has never slowed me down or hindered me in any way in my whole career life, and it's never been a positive business factor either," she adds.

Earned industry respect

Some members of the old boys' club still call her the Beer Babe. But what began as a term of derision has become an expression of grudging admiration.

"Some still call me that – but it's now said with respect after the turnaround," Cascioli smiles, shaking her head.

"And most of them just call me Teresa – they just had to come to terms with the novelty of a lady brewery president," she adds.

"It really doesn't matter who you are. In this highly competitive industry, you still have to prove yourself. And I think we've done that by completely turning this company around."

The return to profits has not been without a great deal of hard work and sacrifice. But Cascioli continually proves her dedication to the difficult task at hand, often putting in 14-hour workdays.

In fact, Cascioli – she's also one of only two female members of the Brewers' Association of Canada – finds her demanding work as President and CEO of Ontario's fourth-largest brewery leaves little time for anything else.

"I'm married to my job," Cascioli admits with a laugh.

"There's no husband, no kids, no pets – I don't even have any plants. Who's got the time to water them?"

Cascioli also finds little time to pursue any hobbies or interests outside of work. Although she keeps beer in her fridge for guests, it's a rare, special occasion when this brewery owner will treat herself to a beer, or any alcoholic drink.

Dedicated to Lakeport's success

No, this determined executive's primary focus is on the business of making Lakeport a successful beverages company.

"I've dedicated the past few years of my life to running this company – everything else comes second," Cascioli asserts.

That approach may wreck havoc with her social life, but there's no question that in lavishing constant attention on her business, she's worked wonders in restoring Lakeport to health and taking the company to the next level of growth in its ongoing evolution.

Lakeport is today a very profitable, highly innovative beverages company that also brings an imaginative approach to promoting its products and achieving impressive growth.

And it's not just a Hamilton success story: Lakeport is the fourth largest brewery in all of Ontario, just behind Sleeman, which in turn is well behind the big two – Molson and Labatt brewers.

Lakeport's beer is available – and enjoys strong sales – across the province. Some brands are also available in other provinces and in the United States. Simply put, Lakeport is a major force in the brewing industry.

How Cascioli came to save and take over Lakeport is a story that begins with her strong background in matters financial and administrative.

A Hamilton girl's success story

Cascioli was born, raised and schooled in Hamilton – "I'm basically a Hamilton girl" – and she has both a gift for understanding financial concepts and an instinctive feel for what does or doesn't sell in Canada's Steel City.

After making her way through the Hamilton school system, Cascioli enrolled at McMaster University in 1979 in her late teens.

She graduated four years later, in 1983, with a four-year Bachelor of Commerce degree.

That same year, Cascioli's joined the staff of the City of Hamilton.

Two years later, Cascioli left the City to join the former Regional Municipality of Hamilton-Wentworth.

She would spend a decade working with the

Region, eventually moving up to become Manager of Finance and Administration.

In her finance manager capacity, the young executive found herself supervising 14 employees and taking on responsibility for a $500-million operating and capital budget.

In addition to managing a half-a-billion-dollar budget, Cascioli also served as Chairman of the Region's Administrative Coordinating Team reporting directly to the Chief Administrative Officer.

The youthful team chairman reported on, and made recommendations concerning, key strategic and cost-saving initiatives for the Region.

Cascioli was also appointed a key negotiator for the Region's outsourcing initiatives.

During this time, she was also active in teaching and developing an array of business and computer courses for Mohawk College of Applied Arts and Technology. Cascioli also taught courses and she advised the college's educational panel on trends in education.

Also on the education front, she wrote and marketed teaching manuals and materials that were subsequently purchased by Hamilton high schools for inclusion in their curriculum.

Forging a private sector career

In 1995, Cascioli left the public sector to accept a new and challenging appointment. She was named Vice-President, Investor Relations, of a large publicly traded private company.

While with the company, Cascioli acted as the

firm's liase with the financial and investment community at large and acquired extensive knowledge of disclosure requirements for publicly traded companies. She also acquired a great deal of stock market intelligence and communication expertise.

Reporting to the Senior Executive Committee, Cascioli worked extensively on the integration of acquired companies.

This was definitely life in the fast lane. But after several years with this major corporation, Cascioli was ready for another challenge.

That challenge arrived in the form of Lakeport Brewing Company, a mid-sized, Hamilton-based brewery that was in very serious financial difficulty.

Taking over Lakeport

Lakeport was under the protection of the Companies Creditors Arrangement Act, legislation dating back to the 1930s Great Depression, which allowed the company refuge from its secured and various unsecured creditors, who were collectively owed $18.2-million.

It had been out of production and in this virtual state of bankruptcy for nearly a year, from November 1998 to September 1999.

In fact, the brewery, which had been operating continuously under various ownerships – including Amstel Breweries – since 1942, was to all real intents and purposes, bankrupt, and in dire need of a saviour.

It found one in Cascioli.

She joined forces with former Philip Services Inc. President and CEO Allen Fracassi to form AlphaCorp Holdings, the investment firm that would take over the financially troubled brewery in 1999 and become the new owner of Lakeport.

After advancing Lakeport $600,000 in working capital and then committing to a $2.5-million equity investment, AlphaCorp received 80 per cent ownership of the troubled brewery from the former owners.

AlphaCorp has since expanded its initial 80 per cent ownership stake to 100 per cent, making the firm the sole owner of Lakeport.

Fracassi, largely a silent investor, is majority owner with 75 per cent of the company while Cascioli owns the remaining 25 per cent and is responsible for running the brewery and beverages businesses.

Saving Lakeport

Cascioli would toil from April 1999 right to November 1999 negotiating the company's exit from bankruptcy, restructuring a pre-existing plan of arrangement, convincing suppliers to again have faith in the brewery and proving to creditors that her approach stood the best possible chance of saving the company.

Much of her time was spent renegotiating the plan of arrangement that was already in place when Cascioli took over.

Under that pre-existing plan of arrangement, creditors were to receive 54 cents of every dollar owed to them.

But Cascioli's analysis showed 54 cents on the dollar couldn't possibly work because "Lakeport couldn't afford to pay this amount and within a matter of months the company would just be bankrupt all over again."

Cascioli did some number crunching and determined that 20 cents on the dollar was the most Lakeport could afford to pay creditors if it was to have a fighting chance at getting – and staying - solvent.

So she prepared a financial analysis, then presented a revised offer to the creditors and delivered a blunt but candid appraisal of Lakeport's tenuous situation.

Tough but simple message

"My message was simple," Cascioli recalls. "I basically informed the creditors that I'd gone over all the numbers and 54 cents couldn't work. They'd either have to accept 20 cents on the dollar or come away with nothing at all. They accepted the new, revised arrangement and we were able to take the next step."

A laugh escapes her lips as Cascioli realizes she's made very difficult negotiations sound a lot easier than they were.

"The truth is that it was a very difficult journey to get to that point. We had to make some hard business decisions and present the situation in a very blunt manner. It's not an easy process. What you need is a stomach made of steel and the mental ability to do what is right for the business even if that's not what is right for the heart."

Cascioli says the next major task was convincing the suppliers and customers to renew their faith in Lakeport.

"We had to re-build our relationships with our suppliers, make them feel good about doing business with us again," she explains.

"When you're dealing with suppliers, employees, customers and others it's necessary for you to maintain a sense of confidence, even if you don't have all the answers," Cascioli confides.

"You have to learn to trust your gut. And you have to make other people believe in you and trust your judgement," she adds.

"It's the only way you can move forward. It's the only way you can accomplish anything. It took a long time, a lot of hard work to get the rebuilding process going – but I'm glad we did."

Lakeport's Lady President

On completing the financial restructuring in November 1999, Teresa Cascioli was named President and Chief Executive Officer of Lakeport Brewing, bringing nearly 20 years of finance, administration, property management and operations experience to the position.

Next, she streamlined operations, eliminating several middle management positions and instituting a just-in-time system for ordering packaging materials.

"As a management team, we brought a sense of urgency to this place that was never here before," she says, noting that one began as a one-woman effort has since evolved into the collective mission of a team of dedicated professionals.

That team has evolved to become a truly impressive collection of experienced professionals, a testimony to Cascioli's efforts to turn Lakeport around and to the company's improving fortunes and ability to attract the best people available.

Team members now include: Chief Operating Officer Russell Tabata, formerly with Molson; Maintenance and Operations Manager Dan Lobeach, formerly with Labatt; Chief Financial Officer Karen Trudell, previously with Cott and Pepsi corporations; and renowned Brewmaster Glenn Fobes, well-respected throughout the brewery business.

Cascioli and her team continue to play an instrumental role in the company's ongoing turnaround, turning her attention to matters of product positioning, marketing and salesmanship.

"By necessity, our focus was initially purely on survival – then profitability," she explains.

"We had to look at every aspect of the business, examine all of the production processes, look at everything that had anything to do with this business and then do whatever was necessary to keep it alive."

A miracle on Burlington Street

Incredibly, Cascioli was able to turn the company's fortunes around to first ensure its survival and then take it to profitability – all in the time span of barely eighteen months. Not that her job is done. She's the first to point out that improving Lakeport's fortunes is very much an ongoing process.

"I'm still getting the full management team in place," Cascioli notes.

"And I'm still going over some basic financial and operational fundamentals – such as the production line configurations. I want to master all of this and make sure that we've put in place the systems that will work best for us."

Thanks to Cascioli's efforts, Lakeport is today

a profitable company that's running three brewing shifts per day, five days a week.

On weekends, Lakeport stops packaging and operates its maintenance and clean-up shifts.

The steady production is needed just to keep up with burgeoning product orders.

And the winner is... Lakeport

Lakeport's impressive, amazing turnaround was recognized in 2001 by the Hamilton Chamber of Commerce, which named Lakeport the winner of its Outstanding Business Achievement award in the Large Business category.

"We're thrilled to have been awarded this honour," Cascioli grins.

"Our employees, customers and suppliers have contributed substantially to Lakeport's success," she asserts with enthusiasm.

"The official recognition is gratifying and it's a real a tribute to the people who have stood by us and believed in us."

With around 240 fulltime employees, Lakeport is capable of brewing an impressive – and thirst-quenching – 8-million cases of 24 per year to line the brewery's walls pending shipment.

That's an impressive potential annual production of 192-million bottles of beer on the wall (and yes, if one of those bottles should happen to fall: 191.999999-million bottles of beer on the wall).

Brewing a lot of great beer

The private company does not release revenue

or profit numbers for competitive reasons. But it's enough to say that Lakeport can, and does, brew an awesome amount of great-tasting premium beer at discount prices.

As Well, Lakeport is capable of blending many million more cases of 'cooler' products for the alternative beverage market.

In operation as a brewery since 1942, the former Amstel Canada plant was bought and then renamed as Lakeport Brewing in 1992.

Making needed changes

After taking over in 1999, Cascioli also took a hard look at product output and decided to change tactics.

"I had to ask myself: Do we really need 24 different brands of beer? Do we really need to be spreading our marketing and production efforts so thinly, promoting so many different brands?"

Cascioli determined Lakeport's strengths lay in the brewery's proven ability to produce a limited number of "value beer" brands – premium-tasting beer at discount prices.

This, of course, includes Lakeport's renowned Honey Lager introduced in the fall of 2002 with the promotional campaign: "A 24 for a 24," giving beer drinkers the bargain opportunity to pick up 24 bottles of this great tasting, premium beer for just $24, a buck-a-bottle rate not seen in many years.

The Honey Lager pitch – and those for Lakeport's other brands – comes as a direct appeal to the resilient budget-market of loyal customers who primarily buy beer at The Beer Store (BRI) to take home with them. To this day, the bulk of Lakeport sales cater to this constituency. Comparatively fewer sales go to bars and restaurants, but Lakeport is taking steps to make its brands available at more locations.

"It's something we're addressing," Cascioli smiles. "We're working on it."

Local offerings...

Locally, you can get a cold Lakeport beer at such Hamilton area establishments as Carmen's Banquet Centre; Hutch's Restaurant; Kings Forest Golf Course; Valentino's Restaurant; Just Greek Restaurant; Texas Border Boot bar & Grill; Fisher's Pier 4 Bar & Grill; Picton Tavern; Southbrook Golf and Country Club; The Hamilton Chamber of Commerce Dining Hall; West Towne tavern; Turtle Jack's bar & Grill; Macassa Yacht Club; Black Forest Inn Tavern; La Cantina; Dodger & Firkin Pub; and Plainsman Tavern.

Lakeport products are also a hit at a number of festival events, including It's Your Festival in Hamilton, Super Latin Fest in Toronto, Ottawa Beer Festival, Buckhorn Beer Festival and the Toronto International Festival of Beer.

Although Lakeport intends to increase its presence in bars, restaurants and festival locations, the company isn't about to lose sight of its primary market: The loyal customer who picks up a case of inexpensive, great-tasting beer and takes it home.

Narrowing the focus

Indeed, Cascioli finds Lakeport's core strengths remain embedded in the offering of a few key brands providing the enviable combination of high quality at low cost.

"We've always tended to cater more to the take-home crowd and less to the pubs," Cascioli notes, "and I don't see that changing anytime soon although we'll continue to reach out to the beer market in restaurants and bars."

She also saw these core strengths as key to Lakeport's survival and long-term prosperity.

"I realized the quickest way to turning things around was by narrowing our marketing approach," Cascioli explains.

Great beer at a great price

"We rationalized all of our various brands to gain some needed operations efficiency," she adds, noting the Lakeport brands – Pilsener, Light, Dry, Strong and Ice – are now marketed together as a family of Lakeport beers.

All of these brands – available at all Beer Store and LCBO locations across Ontario – offer premium taste at value pricing that is $3 to $4 per case of 24 below competing national brands.

Lakeport's brands are also available at the company's own Cold Beer Store, right beside its world class brewing facility at Burlington Street East, Hamilton.

The Cold Beer Store is open Mondays through Saturday's from 10 am to 6 pm and on Sundays from noon to 6 pm.

In addition to its family of Lakeport brands, Lakeport brews Steeler Lager – a tip of the hat to

Hamilton in bottles or eye-catching 'cold steel' cans – and Mongoose Malt Liquor, a strong beer with 8 per cent alcohol by volume that's earned it the moniker "The Beer that Bites Back."

Mongoose, available in convenient, quick-chill 32 fl oz. cans is also sold outside Ontario in several American states; while a 950-ml king can is available in the Western Canadian provinces of Alberta and Manitoba.

Driving sales of all of Lakeport's brands is lower pricing levels that allow the consumer to save while making no quality sacrifice whatsoever.

"Beer is a very elastic product," Cascioli explains, "because sales can easily go up or down."

"Any price decrease – even a slight decrease – brings large increases in sales volume."

Bravo to four Brava brands

Lakeport's own proprietary beer brands also include the Brava Cerveza brands, the wildly popular, authentic Mexican tasting "beer of summer," which is also available in Brava Lime, Negra and Light versions.

Lakeport routinely receives letters and comments from Mexican beer aficionados on how authentically Mexican tasting Brava beer truly is.

Brava also looks Mexican, thanks to the product label redesign Cascioli ordered after she decided to re-launch the "beer of summer."

Cascioli contacted Rossi Piedmonte Design and explained she wanted a label that would give anyone who looked at it a sense of "the sun, the heat, the Aztecs, Mexico."

Armed with Cascioli's concept, the highly creative marketing firm came up with a striking label that conjured up all of those images.

The newly revamped Brava proved a hit and it immediately quadrupled its sales. And sales have been further fuelled with the introduction of Brava Lime, Negra and Light versions of this popular brand.

Highly effective marketing

Lakeport's marketing approach is modest compared to its big competitors, but the approach is extremely focused and effective.

In addition to its eye-catching labels and prominent presence at many summer festivals, Lakeport sports highly visible painted images of its brands on big beer-transport trucks plying Ontario's highways and byways.

As well, the family of Lakeport brands is marketed as a group while a separate advertising campaign is used to bolster the presence of Brava.

Like Mongoose, Brava is also available in several American states, including Pennsylvania, New York, Texas, California and Florida.

In response to growing demand for great Canadian beer from U.S. distributors, Lakeport also brews a couple of brands exclusively for the American market: These include Lakeport Premium Lager. Available in 12-oz and 32-oz cans, it's a full-bodied, rich-tasting Canadian lager that's a favourite with American beer drinkers.

And, there's Lakeport's even more overtly cultural foray into the U.S. market: Truly Canadian Lager Beer.

Beyond the fresh, clean Canadian taste, the labels bear the familiar - to Canadians - likeness of Canada's first Prime Minister.

Below Sir John A. MacDonald's image is his name and lifespan – 1815-1891. Truly Canadian is available in 12-oz cans, by six-pack or tray of 24.

Closer to home, Lakeport also services a huge market for private label non-alcoholic beer bands in many major grocery store chains, including A&P, Ultramart, Sobeys, Provigo, Loblaws and Fortinos. It is the leading supplier on non-alcohol beer products for all of Canada.

A profitable blend

To meet the demand, under Cascioli's leadership, Lakeport's brewing facility has been returned to the exclusive production of beer ranging from non-alcoholic to high-alcohol strong brands.

But Lakeport also makes extensive use of its new state-of-the-art Blending Facility to service its many co-pack clients.

After the new blending facility was started up in 2000, it immediately allowed Lakeport to substantially raise its production capacity.

The facility also has maximum flexibility and accuracy in batch, semi-batch and continuous blending of products to three packaging lines.

This fully automated system also allows cooler recipes to be selected from an on-screen menu.

Once the selection is made, the ingredients are rapidly blended and processed into the finished product.

While one cooler is being prepared, the system

automatically cleans and prepares another part of the system for the next product.

"The new facility allows us to blend with accuracy and uniformity on a consistent basis," Cascioli explains.

"Change-over between products is very fast and efficient."

Huge output capacity

The new blending facility when combined with the brewery infrastructure, gives Lakeport a huge output capacity that allows the beverage company to met the needs of an expanding customer base for alcoholic and non-alcoholic products.

Cascioli observes that the integration of the brewery with the new blending operation also gives Lakeport the "truly unique opportunity to offer our existing and future clients a wide choice of blending and processing operations from which to produce their products."

"And that's a terrific capability no other Canadian co-packer currently offers," she adds.

Yes, in addition to being a major brewery for great-tasting beers, Lakeport is now very much a leading co-manufacturer of alcoholic and non-alcoholic spirit and malt-based cooler products, including a popular lemony flavoured cooler.

As well, Lakeport produces and markets the fast-selling Mott's Clamato Ready-To-Drink Caesar – Original and Extra Spicy – for the Mott's Inc., a subsidiary of the giant Cadbury Schweppes company based in England.

Among the attractions the cooler firms have for using Lakeport's services is the Hamilton company's ability to do it all, from mixing, blending and bottling the product to marketing it, and getting it placed on store shelves.

Indeed, Cascioli observes that turning to Lakeport to handle their non-beer products, the cooler producers have a range of options they can choose from.

Menu of services make Caesar king

"We offer a whole menu of services," she proudly asserts, "including our laboratory services, marketing graphics, LCBO placement, logistics help, materials and packaging and marketing."

"For example, Mott's didn't have a sales organization to promote its Clamato cocktails, so they asked us to market Mott's Caesars. And our sales team is Mott's exclusive sales agent in Ontario for the LCBO."

However, as lucrative as the market is for handling the products of others, Cascioli notes "your profit margins are higher on your own brands because you own them outright."

With that in mind, Cascioli immediately placed a growing emphasis on beer production.

Today, beer accounts for fully 50 per cent of production, up from 25 per cent when she took over.

The remaining production is now dedicated to co-packaging the products of other, client companies. The combined brewery and blending facilities have given Lakeport a solid standing in both beer and cooler markets. It's an enviable – but also necessary – position to hold in today's highly competitive marketplace.

Lakeport versus everyone

Asked who her competitors are, Cascioli replies: "Everybody."

"We're not just competing with the other brewers, but also with all of the alternatives to beer itself, such as the ready-to-drink cocktails and coolers," she notes.

"Our biggest challenge is to continually provide great-tasting, value-priced, alternative choices for anyone, anywhere desiring an alcohol-based drink."

Long-term stability

Cascioli also brought additional stability to Lakeport in the fall of 2000 by securing a five-year contract with the Teamsters Local Union 938, a union she praises for its willingness to work with the company to achieve a fair and productivity-friendly, long-term working agreement.

"The Teamsters have been absolutely terrific," she says, adding "and I think the union also appreciates the fact that we try to run the company in a very fair manner."

Craig McInnes, business representative for Teamsters, agrees: "Teamsters Local Union 938 is please to participate in Lakeport's growth initiatives," says McInnes.

"We are proud to be part of this dynamic growth-oriented company."

Lakeport also has a number of promotional items, including boxed golf balls and Brava baseball caps. You can also get Lakeport golf tees, pens, pins and tee shirts.

The company invites corporations hosting social events to contact the brewery so that Lakeport can support their event with great giveaway items.

Beer and gear online

You can even order "beer and gear" online from Lakeport's Website: www.lakeportbeverage.ca where you'll find a virtual catalogue to peruse.

Order a case of 24 and it will be delivered by Canada Post Priority Courier the next business day.

An add-on cost of up to $30 may be applied to cover shipping and handling, making this type of order convenient, but expensive.

The online service is just another facet of a remarkable business that has rapidly evolved into more than a brewery, more than a beverages company, more than a marketing firm, more than a distributor. It is all of these things and more.

And it is Cascioli's vision that has made Lakeport far more than the sum of its many parts.

Driven by vision to succeed

It is her vision that has reshaped this company into a vibrant industry leader, an innovator, major employer and positive economic force in the community it calls home.

Cascioli can take pride in reinventing Lakeport

as a far more innovative entity than it had ever been in its past lives. "Lakeport is now selling its capabilities, as opposed to just selling its brands," Cascioli asserts with a smile.

"We're very pleased with our proprietary brands, but we also have a strategic focus on customer service and on selling our capabilities to our customers," she adds.

"And that, more than anything else, should keep moving this company forward."

Teresa Cascioli's tips for success

1. Decide what you want to achieve and clearly define your goals.

2. Dedicate yourself to achieving your goals and be prepared to work many long hours.

3. Set out a compelling vision of success and gain the co-operation of others to achieve it.

4. Be prepared to make the tough but needed decisions to advance your business dream.

5. Determine what your customers want and tailor your product or services accordingly.

6. Give praise whenever it's due. Keep your staff motivated to continue performing well.

7. Find out who your competitors are and figure out how you can offer something more to customers than they can. Make your competitors' weaknesses your strengths.

8. Develop an innovative marketing approach that will set you apart from the competition.

9. Think outside the box. Just because your firm started out doing one thing doesn't mean it must forever limit itself to that single product or service.

10. Achieve new growth by expanding your business horizons. Seek out new markets for whatever product or service your provide.

11. Be brutally honest, whether the content of your message is positive or negative. This way, people will always know exactly where you stand. They'll also know there's no hidden agenda or attempt to mislead.

12. Build a team of talented, dedicated people who can contribute their expertise and help you take your business to the next level.

Hamilton's commercial core

Chapter Nine

Hamilton Chamber of Commerce
Helping Businesses Succeed

"The chamber has always been front and centre when it comes to addressing legitimate concerns of business and the community."

- John Dolbec

At a Glance: The Hamilton Chamber of Commerce

Hamilton Chamber of Commerce
Claim to fame: The leading source businesses turn to for networking opportunities and advice. The Hamilton Chamber's slogan is "Creating Business Opportunities," and it has been helping businesses achieve their dreams since it was founded in 1845.
Financial Data: The Chamber administers an annual budget in the range of $2-million. It is a self-supporting, not-for-profit entity that also runs a very popular dining facility: The Waterfront Dining Club. As well, the Chamber produces a directory and other publications at a modest profit.
For More information:
Contact: Hamilton Chamber of Commerce
Phone: (905) 522-1151
Fax: (905) 522-1154.
Address: 555 Bay Street North, Hamilton, Ontario, L8L 1H1 (foot of Bay Street at Hamilton Harbour).
Email: hdcc@hamiltonchamber.on.ca
Internet: www.hamiltonchamber.on.ca

Chapter Nine

Hamilton Chamber of Commerce
Helping Businesses Succeed

Businesses serious about success rely on a key organization for help: the Hamilton Chamber of Commerce.

Indeed, the Chamber's slogan: "Creating Business Opportunities," speaks to the services it's provided for nearly 160 years.

Chamber-created opportunities include the frequent chances to network.
Members are provided with a number of catered business forums – most of them free of charge – throughout the year to promote their goods and services to 1,700 fellow Chamber members.
But the opportunities don't end there.

As Chamber Chief Executive Officer John Dolbec notes: "The benefits are extensive – what you get out of the Chamber depends, in part, in what you happen to put into it."

"We have numerous breakfast meetings, special events and committees you can get involved with, and your involvement can bring you a good deal of insight and information on a range of topics," Dolbec adds in an interview at Chamber headquarters, at the foot of Bay Street in a building the organization shares with the Royal Hamilton Yacht Club.

"Each Chamber member has an individual reason for joining the organization and we attempt to respond to those needs as individually as possible," Dolbec says, rising from his chair to savour an enviable view of ducks and sailboats gliding serenely on the calm recreational waters that shimmer in the sun.

"The mission of the Chamber as the voice of ethical enterprise is that we are committed to making Hamilton a great place to live, work, play and invest, while recognizing the importance of the individual as the most significant contributor to achieving community objectives."

A history of promoting commerce

The Chamber's ongoing success is pegged to its central role in fostering the growth of Hamilton's traditional role as a major commercial centre.

Indeed, from very early in its history, before steel and heavy industry, Hamilton was a thriving centre of trade and commerce - a proud heritage that continues through to this day.

In fact, in 1845 – a year before the Hamilton community was truly and duly incorporated as the City of Hamilton – the bustling community had by that point already established the Hamilton Board of Trade, the business-promoting forerunner of today's Hamilton Chamber of Commerce.

And the importance of business people in making a difference wasn't lost on the trade board's first-ever president, Isaac Buchanan, a visionary who noted back in 1845 "without the committed leadership of those who strive to build an economy, our community will cease to strengthen and grow."

As well, the Hamilton Board of Trade had been an early supporter of free trade with the United States, although it reversed that position in 1910 to an effort to protect Hamilton manufacturers. Almost 80 years later the chamber would again support free trade with the Americans, indeed the world at large.

In 1903, the board pushed for numerous civic improvements such as additional drinking fountains. It also formed an alliance with Hamilton's Trades and Labour Council to arbitrate an end to a very costly Teamsters strike hurting the local economy.

Chamber helped bring McMaster here

And in 1920 another milestone was reached when the board reconstituted itself as the Hamilton Chamber of Commerce and quickly took on such successful projects as relocating McMaster University from Toronto to Hamilton and bringing about the welcome establishment of the Chedoke Golf Course.

During the Great Depression of the 1930s, the

chamber demonstrated considerable compassion for the less fortunate members of Hamilton society. The chamber initiated a system of garden plots allowing the unemployed to grow produce. And it raised funds to cover rent owed by needy citizens.

From 1939-1945, the chamber supported the Second World War effort by organizing massive donations of foodstuffs and gifts for the City of Hamilton Tiger Squadron, a bomber squadron manned by local volunteers fighting overseas.

As Hamilton celebrated its centennial in 1946, the chamber played its usual active role, promoting, among other events, the first Miss Canada Pageant.

During the 1980s, the chamber could be found supporting the Corporate Challenge fitness and fun event, Crime Stoppers and a Chinese chamber to attract Asian investment.

A prominent voice of business

In the 1990s, the chamber continued its active role, speaking out on tax issues, government budgets and legislative concerns while bringing a lengthy list of prominent business leaders and speakers to the city to address everything from business strategies for success to exports and international trade.

During the 1996 Hamilton Sesquicentennial year, the chamber contributed enormously to making this a successful year.

Among the Chamber's many achievements was the introduction of a striking commemorative Sesquicentennial coin created by Ancaster sculptor Elizabeth Holbrook.

Also in the mid-1990s, the Globe & Mail's Report on Business magazine ranked the Hamilton area as one of the best communities in which one can do business in Canada.

Clearly the Hamilton Chamber's oft-said message – that Hamilton is a great place to do business – seems to finally be getting out to the national media.

The need to repeat this message to wider audiences has been taken to heart by the chamber's many members who play a leadership role in building our economic region.

And this historic role is now being championed by a new generation of chamber members, many of them young entrepreneurs and small business people.

The rise of small business

Dolbec also notes the Chamber has experienced first-hand the rise of small businesses as the Canadian economy's leading source of new jobs and opportunities.

"An overwhelming number of our members are small businesses," he acknowledges.

"At one time the major industries accounted for the bulk of jobs, but that's changed," he adds.

"Small businesses are where you'll find the most employment growth. There are more small businesses around today than ever before – and that's certainly reflected in our membership. The trend started in the mid-1990s and has continued."

Dolbec says the mid-1990s was also when the Chamber began targeting small businesses by starting programs that catered to one-man outfits to small firms with 100 or fewer employees.

In fact, Dolbec observes that most of the growth in manufacturing jobs has occurred outside the steel industry via an abundance of small manufacturers each employing fewer than 100 people. "We're also seeing growth in services in general, high tech industries, bio-technology jobs and information services," he adds.

"And entrepreneurs are creating many of these new jobs. People getting into business on their own are creating their own job plus additional jobs for other people."

Small businesses, including home-based businesses, now constitute the fastest growing source of members at the chamber and this has led the venerable organization to devote more of its time and energy representing the concerns of small business. That change in approach reflects a societal reality: Small businesses dominate the new age economy.

Strength in diversity

Dolbec observes that small business remains the primary source of new jobs "and that's probably a good thing. It would seem to be healthier to depend on many small companies for jobs than rely on one or two big firms to create employment."

He says that with growing numbers of entrepreneurs and small businesses starting up and thriving, the economy is becoming more and more diverse.

"Diversity is a real strength. You're not as dependent on one or two sectors of the economy or one or two companies to keep you going. Economic changes that hurt some companies may not hurt others. Having a diversified economy means you're in a better position to withstand an inevitable recession."

One component of Hamilton's diversified economy is its vibrant transportation section, including the busiest port in the St. Lawrence Seaway system, and an airport that continues to grow and expand.

"What's happening at the airport has just been phenomenal – it's now the number one airport in Canada for freight," Dolbec asserts, "and I've seen forecasts that call for more than 11,000 employees working at the airport within the next five years."

The construction sector is also booming, with a record $100-million in building permits issued for the month of July 2002.

Dolbec says diversity is just one of the competitive advantages enjoyed by the Greater Hamilton area.

Many hometown advantages

"Some of our other strengths include the ability of many of our companies to make specialized products and services for niche markets," he notes.

"We also benefit from a low-valued dollar which helps our exports compete abroad, our low real estate costs, and our lower costs of doing business," he adds.

"When you look at all of our strengths, it's apparent that we're well-positioned to weather economic downturns and thrive in economic recoveries."

Dolbec notes the Chamber and city of Hamilton

have always been inextricably tied to one another.

"The chamber has always been front and centre when it comes to addressing the legitimate concerns of business and the community," notes Dolbec.

"Our history and our future are closely tied to making our business community – and the wider community beyond that – as successful as possible."

Hamilton much more than steel

Dolbec notes that visitors to Hamilton are often struck by how attractive the city is. Its vistas, parks and pleasant neighbourhoods can quickly dispel any last, lingering, outdated images of Hamilton as a gritty centre of heavy industry.

Yes, the city is proud of its heavy industrial heritage, prouder still that it remains home to many heavy and light industries.

And Canada's Steel City is more than a little proud that it's home to the nation's two largest steelmakers, Stelco Inc. and Dofasco Inc.

Many millions of dollars spent on technology investments have made the steel giants efficient, high tech companies that produce more tons of steel per man-hour than most of their rivals.

Yet, while the steel industry and support industries remain a major source of employment in Hamilton, the city's economy has steadily diversified over the years. The health care services sector now employs more people in Hamilton than any other sector.

And this is one of the most liveable cities in the world, boasting an abundance of parks, many festivals, a recreational waterfront, relatively little real traffic congestion, less pollution than many other major cities, low unemployment, affordable housing and an overall quality of life that is the envy of many communities.

By the late 1990s, the population of the former Hamilton-Wentworth region approached 470,000 people – more than 320,000 of them residing in Hamilton itself.

A growing metropolis

And by 2002, following the amalgamation of Hamilton and Wentworth as the new single City of Hamilton, the total population exceeded 500,000 people – all of them residing in the now expanded city.

Hamilton was a full-fledged metropolis of more than half-a-million people – and growing fast.

Add in the interdependent, interconnected regions of Halton and Niagara and it's apparent that Hamilton is the economic and geographic hub of an economic region of more than 1 million people.

The borders of this vast economic region are somewhat elastic and can include Haldimand-Norfolk lands to the south, Grimsby to the east and Brant County to the West, increasing the population to more than 1.2 million.

Hamilton is at the heart of a community of communities, a Hamilton-centred hinterland of shared geography and economic interests.

And this economic region boasts a highly diversified economy, including everything from soft fruit growing and winemaking, to heavy industry and high tech companies.

The chamber is now focusing on how Hamilton

can best take advantage of its enviable position at the hub of one of North America's most densely populated international markets. Within a 500-mile radius of Hamilton, about a day's truck drive, is a total market population of 120 million people.

"People are beginning to get the message that, as proud as we are of our steel industry, there's a lot more to Hamilton than steel," Dolbec notes.
Catalano notes international business ties are being developed through the Bordernet organization promoting importing and exporting with the U.S.

Massive growth in exports

Just a few years ago, Hamilton companies exported more than 50 per cent of the many goods and services produced in this city.

Today, exports account for fully two-thirds of local output, with most of these goods and services bound for the United States.

"The U.S. is the biggest recipient of our exports," Dolbec observes. "There's a huge amount of cross border trade that takes place here."

Brownfields, vacated or underused lands that once housed industries, are giving rise to many new companies and new sources of employment.

One of the most striking examples of a virtual brownfield being transformed into a bustling centre of commerce can be found on Hamilton's industrialized waterfront.

An entire community of small businesses has now found a home in old, previously vacated factories and warehouses once were used by industrial giants.

This industrial park space is now being leased by the Hamilton Harbour Commissioners at low rental rates to an array of tenants, including De Feo's Auto Service Ltd., which has expanded to include several adjoining service bays in a former industrial warehouse. Numerous other businesses have long made their home in the immediate area, including McKeil marine and Heddle Marine.

Benefiting in the information age

The new, information age, economy is also bringing new job opportunities. Fibre optic wire firms have made the downtown core a leader among inner city cores for its ability to offer high-speed Internet even in old buildings. This growth has also meant hundreds of jobs.

Efforts are also underway to develop Hamilton's 'smart community' potential, via uplinks to satellite linkages, allowing doctors many miles apart to have a fibre optic consultation on television screens. A diagnosis or patient information can be shared instantly via multimedia, telecommunication uplink technology.

Dolbec notes two other firms, Cogeco and Union Energy, have joined Media Express in establishing call centres in Hamilton.

"Altogether, between the three companies, we're looking at something in order of 900 jobs," Dolbec smiles.

"That level of job growth is impressive," he adds. "It means that even with the lose of hundreds at Procter & Gamble, M.A. Henry and J. I. Case, we still have a net gain of jobs from call centres alone."

That such dynamic endeavours would locate in downtown Hamilton shouldn't be surprising. The city's core boasts an abundance of available space at some relatively low rates.

Although still struggling in places, Hamilton's downtown is seeing many millions of dollars in ongoing investment, including the renovated John Sopinka Unified Family Court House, renovations to the old Spectator building and the development of downtown condominium buildings.

The Royal Connaught, Howard Johnson Plaza Hotel has also undergone millions of dollars worth of renovations and the Sheraton Hamilton is playing a vital economic role in revitalizing the downtown core.

"There are great opportunities downtown," Dolbec notes. "The realty prices are low, the problems are solvable and the potential is great."

Co-ordinated effort

Dolbec also observes the community has become a well-organized whole with once-distant institutions regularly conferring with each other to devise programs that can best exploit the impressive new commercial and employment opportunities a changing business world is offering.

The Chamber is in regular contact with the Hamilton Economic Development Department, Mohawk College, McMaster University and HIT (Hamilton Incubator for Technology), which is nearly fully leased and serves as an incubator for start-up high-tech firms.

Dolbec points out that the Chamber worked

closely with Hamilton's Economic Development Department in the drafting of a new strategic plan to guide the city into a prosperous future of growth.

Co-operative relationship

"It's a very co-operative relationship," Dolbec notes. There's a common desire to work together to solve our problems and help our community prosper. "

Dolbec also asserts: "And there's a very strong sense of everyone working together to face common challenges – you don't find that in many communities."

"In fact," he continues, "one of the really beautiful things I love about Hamilton is that this is a very close-knit community. There's a lot of warm-hearted, generous people who don't hesitate to roll up their sleeves and work together to help the community prosper and grow."

Not that there aren't problems.

"We're frequently faced with shortages of skilled labour," Dolbec notes. "Anyone with marketable skills – particularly skilled trades people such as tool and die makers, electricians, carpenters and machinists - are finding it relatively easy to find work," he adds.

Dolbec notes many skilled trades people are middle-aged or older and there is no new generation of skilled trades to replace them.

"The demand for new skilled trades people is there – the supply isn't. It's important that we find ways, develop programs, to create the skills that are needed in our community."

Dolbec notes Ontario Flightcraft could have expanded but it was unable to take on more orders because the company needed 45 to 50 skilled people – air mechanics for its aircraft maintenance and repair facility – and couldn't find them. Instead, the firm turned away the orders and laid off some staff.

"It's unfortunate that some firms are losing business because they lack skilled trades people and the jobs are going begging."

Dolbec says the Ontario-wide shortage of skilled trades presents a huge opportunity for those people willing to learn a trade.

Trades shortage presents opportunity

"Unfortunately, not many young people are eager to get into the trades. There seems to be a stigma about working with your hands, despite the fact that many of these jobs have starting salaries of $50,000 or more."

He says Europe's strengthening economies have made immigration less of a solution than ever to the skilled trades shortage.

"Business hasn't done enough to train future generations – it's coming back to haunt us," he adds.

"However, there are genuine efforts underway to address this problem. Businesses are working closely with community colleges to create and promote programs to create the skills."

Dolbec takes heart in the work being done to ensure a new generation has the option of going into a trade.

"There's more of a willingness and effort to address these problems than there perhaps has been in some time."

Dolbec says Hamilton's favourable position is owed in part to it geographical location in the huge Southern Ontario market with access to the even greater U.S. market.

Benefiting from free trade

He says both the Canada-U.S. Free Trade Agreement and the subsequent North American Free Trade Agreement have succeeded in giving Hamilton companies relatively unfettered access to the American market.

"There were concerns from some that free trade would cost jobs. What we've found instead is that free trade has saved jobs and created jobs."

Dolbec observes one of the main beneficiaries of the FTA has been Hamilton's manufacturing sector.

"Hamilton still has a strong manufacturing sector," he notes, adding that the service sector is experiencing phenomenal growth.

"Services oriented companies have gone from accounting for 34 per cent of the chamber's membership to more than 50 per cent," he notes.

Yet manufacturing remains a strong source of employment. "That may sound surprising," Dolbec admits, "because Stelco and Dofasco only employ half the number of people they employed in the early 1980s. But a lot of the new jobs are coming from young and growing manufacturers."

"For example," he explains, "Décor Pre-cast, which makes patio stones, has gone from 40 employees to 130 and its sales to the U.S. have quintupled in past four to five years."

Dolbec also notes the city's entire economy has diversified. After years of downsizing, the big industries seem to have found an employment balance and they remain a secure source of existing jobs. The Manufacturing sector is vibrant, the health care and education sectors are growing and the entire services sector is expanding.

Low unemployment

Hamilton still boasts one of the lowest unemployment rates in all of Canada as one advantage among many.

As Dolbec notes: "We have the lowest unemployment rates anywhere, a highly skilled labour force, a great quality of life and, compared to many other centres, the cost of doing business here is low. We also offer fast, convenient access to other markets in Toronto and the U.S."

"In every area you can possible think of, Hamilton continues to provide an enviable place to live, work and play."

The Chamber's tips for success:

1. Join the Hamilton Chamber of Commerce and start enjoying its many benefits.
2. Consider participating in Chamber events and joining committees of interest.
3. Take part in chamber forums and be sure that you network – hand out business cards and become known.
4. Contribute your time to the Chamber and other worthy causes. The more you put in the more you're likely to benefit.
5. Tap into the expertise offered through the Chamber's access to many speakers and prominent business leaders.
6. Research and define the market you want to serve with your goods or products.
7. Determine what your client's needs, wants are. Go the extra mile to delight them.
8. Treat others well: Return all phone calls promptly. Service your customers well.
9. Map out your business plan and strategy for achieving success – then follow it.
10. Always strive to do better, to achieve new things, to always expand your horizons, to constantly reach for new levels of success.

Michael G. DeGroote

Chapter Ten

Michael G. DeGroote

Builder of Business Empires

"As big providers keep raising the bar for the size of firms they'll serve, a lot more firms are left out… We're happy to live off these leftovers. By taking over back office paperwork, we're helping these smaller firms become competitive and grow."

- Michael G. DeGroote

At a Glance: Michael G. DeGroote:

Michael G. DeGroote
Age: 69
Title: Chairman, CBIZ (Century Business Services Inc.), President, Westbury (Bermuda) Limited, director, AutoNation.
Claim to fame: From humble beginnings, language difficulties and limited education, DeGroote overcame bankruptcies to build Laidlaw Inc. into a multi-billion-dollar firm. After selling his Laidlaw shares for over $500-million, DeGroote moved to Bermuda where he's building new business empires.
Financial Data: DeGroote is a wealthy man. CBIZ has annual revenue exceeding $500-million US and assets totalling more than $500-million US.
Personal: Resides in Bermuda, but enjoys return visits to Canada and spending time with his sons Tim, Michael and Gary; daughter Joni and his grandchildren. He also enjoys boating, but his biggest passion is business deal-making.

Chapter Ten

Michael G. DeGroote

Building Business Empires

Michael G. DeGroote: Successful business leader; inspiration to generations of entrepreneurs; one of the world's wealthiest people.

And, from his home amid the leafy palm trees and gentle breezes of sunny Bermuda, DeGroote is building new business empires and inspiring new generations of entrepreneurs.

DeGroote, now in his late sixties, started out as a small businessman.

Now he's reaching out to small companies and helping them grow: His newest business empire takes over much of the entrepreneurs' paperwork to free up time for them to pursue their business vision and goals.

Through CBIZ (Century Business Services Inc.), DeGroote has become a major provider of payroll, accounting and other business-oriented services to small firms that had long been virtually ignored by his competitors.

And in helping these small to mid-sized firms employing five to 500 people, CBIZ Chairman Michael G. DeGroote is tapping into an underdeveloped but lucrative market for outsourcing administrative services, worth $250-billion US.

Growth through acquisitions

Through a series of acquisitions, CBIZ now owns numerous accounting, insurance and benefits firms.

Today, through its 76 business units and more than 200 offices in 33 states, Washington, D.C., and Toronto, DeGroote's fast-growing CBIZ firm provides one-stop shopping for over 110,000 smaller firms, taking care of their payroll, hiring, firing, benefits, medical insurance, accounting and other paperwork matters, freeing firms to focus their energy on their business.

And CBIZ, with annual revenue exceeding $500-million US, is one of the largest accounting firms in the United States. It provides services through a cross-serving network of member firms, following a hub and spokes concept, and employing enviable benefits of scale.

For many years, all of these services have been available to big companies through a number of giant providers that tend to simply ignore the smaller firms.

DeGroote is now providing the same services to the smaller firms, steadily mining a virtually untapped market.

He's also on the board of directors for AutoNation, Inc., the largest automotive retailer in the United States. The firm owns and operates over 370 new vehicle franchises from dealership locations in 17 states.

AutoNation's revenue of $12.6-billion US in 1998 had grown to $20-billion US by 2001.

Success story began in Canada

All of this follows DeGroote's earlier success in Canada, where he built the Laidlaw firm into a multi-billion-dollar corporate giant.

In recognition of DeGroote's profound and enduring contribution to Canada, he was awarded the Order of Canada.

He also holds an honorary law degree from McMaster University, which also renamed its business school as: The Michael G. DeGroote School of Business, in recognition of his generous financial support.

DeGroote's success is indeed the stuff of legends. Forbes magazine's International 500 list routinely ranks him as one of the richest people in the world. Forbes estimates his fortune at over $1.2 billion US (that's approaching $2 billion CDN).

In fact, DeGroote is also routinely ranked as one of Canada's wealthy elite, along with Galen Weston, Kenneth Thomson, the Irving family and Charles Bronfman.

Of these billionaire Canadians, only one, Michael DeGroote, did not inherit his wealth.

He earned it. And DeGroote's ability to amass a vast fortune by his own hands is all the more impressive given the obstacles he faced in his youth.

Born in war-torn Belgium

Born on a farm in West Flanders, Belgium, in 1933, Michael George DeGroote saw his childhood stripped of innocence by the brutality of World War II.

He was just 14 years old when his family left war-torn Belgium for Canada in 1948, settling on a tobacco farm in Langton, Ontario, about 60 miles south-west of Hamilton.

"Belgium was in major disarray, caused by the Second World War and there was talk then that there could be a third war," DeGroote recalls, in his gravel voice revealing the barest trace of a Flemish accent. "I couldn't speak much English back then except for 'yes', 'okay' and a few swear words."

Language Barrier

Faced with a language barrier and a difficult period of adjustment, DeGroote took advantage of a now defunct Ontario law allowing youth as young as 14 to drop out of school. He has never attended an Ontario school.

Yet, despite his obvious subsequent success, the hard-driving businessman still regrets never having extended his formal education beyond the equivalent of Grade 10.

"I think it meant that I had to work twice as hard to succeed," DeGroote asserts.

"There really is no substitute for a good education," adds the founder of the Michael G. DeGroote School of Business, who has generously supported the Business School at McMaster University.

Entrepreneurial spirit emerges

DeGroote's own entrepreneurial spirit emerged just a few years after he arrived in Canada.

In the early 1950s, an 18-year-old DeGroote bought his first truck – a two-ton army vehicle – and went into business hauling manure from the London area to farms in Langton and Tillsonburg.

But many decades later, Canadian Business magazine would honour DeGroote's humble business beginnings: The magazine not only listed the wealthiest Canadians – DeGroote was ranked 15th – but it also listed Canada's billionaires in the category of starting out with the worst first job.

First job stunk

DeGroote was awarded first prize for having started out hauling manure. No one else even came close to winning this dubious honour.

"It was honest work, but my first job sure stunk," DeGroote recalls with a smile.

By the mid-1950s, DeGroote had expanded his first business to include a second truck and a tractor to work area farms plus four gravel dump trucks to work a Woodstock quarry.

And by 1957, he had expanded his fleet to about 30 trucks and formed Langton Contracting Co. Ltd., setting up operations at Elliot Lake, then a booming uranium-mining town.

Although the Elliot Lake location was seen as advantageous at the time, the fateful decision to set up operations in that mining town would later come back to haunt him.

Two years later, DeGroote made a now legendary acquisition when he borrowed $75,000 to buy Robert Laidlaw's Laidlaw Transport Ltd.

DeGroote's then newly purchased Laidlaw company was back then a small Hagersville-based trucking business, with a tiny fleet of only a few trucks.

DeGroote builds up Laidlaw

Although the name 'Laidlaw' would take on much greater significance in later years, back in 1959 it was very much a small business when the new owner took it over and added it to his Langton Contracting business.

DeGroote's plan was to expand through the acquisition of other companies.

But DeGroote's emerging business empire was dealt a sudden, staggering body blow when an unforeseen plunge in the uranium market prompted an exodus of people and business from Elliot Lake.

The population of the northern Ontario town fell to 6,000 people from 28,000. DeGroote's own fortunes fell just as fast.

DeGroote tried to rebuild the business in Sudbury but the financial wounds were too deep. In

1962, Langton Contracting went bankrupt, owing nearly $500,000 to 175 creditors.

A year later DeGroote also declared personal bankruptcy with liabilities exceeding $450,000.

"I kept Laidlaw, but I went from driving Cadillacs and living in a rather nice house to driving a rusty, used car and living in a small rented place," he recalls.

"The experience of bankruptcy has taught me a lesson that's stayed with me – you can't overextend yourself financially," adds DeGroote whose subsequent corporate empires have been free of the heavy debt loads that have caused the fall of lesser giants.

A man of his word

Just four months after declaring bankruptcy, DeGroote was discharged, allowing him to get back in business with a clean slate.

It wasn't easy, but within the next six years, DeGroote paid back all his creditors.

"I know that legally I didn't have to pay people back but I did because I felt it was the right thing to do," he explains.

"These people lent me money in good faith and I felt responsible regardless of what the bankruptcy laws said."

It was the right thing to do – and it earned DeGroote an enduring reputation as a man of his word, someone who doesn't forget the people who believe in him.

Laidlaw, purchased with borrowed money, was far from being an overnight success story.

"It was so heavily leveraged that it was six years before I could draw a salary – and it wasn't until I took it public in 1969 that I could get any money out," recalls the former Dundas resident who took 30 years from his 1959 purchase of Laidlaw to gradually build the company into a $2 billion-a-year corporate giant.

Thirty-year overnight success story

"I guess you could say Laidlaw really was an overnight success story – it just took 30 years to make that second billion overnight," he jokes.

All told, Canada's Grand Acquisitor purchased some 500 companies on Laidlaw's behalf, transforming Laidlaw in the process.

Laidlaw, which moved its Hagersville headquarters to Hamilton and later Burlington, grew to become the third-largest waste management firm in North America.

At the same time, Laidlaw was also the second-largest hazardous waste company and largest operator of school buses.

Bermuda-bound after selling shares

In 1988, DeGroote stunned Canada's financial community by selling his many Laidlaw Inc. shares to Canadian Pacific for $500-million.

That same year, Laidlaw had been hailed as the number one growth stock in Canada – for the 17th year in a row.

DeGroote stayed on as chief executive officer of Laidlaw for two more years.

And Laidlaw continued to grow by leaps and bounds to achieve market capitalization of over $6 billion (fifth-largest in Canada) by the time DeGroote resigned in mid-1990.

DeGroote took a huge tax hit – but it was also his last tax hit.

He gathered his fortune together and moved to a new home amid the palm trees and gentle breezes of Bermuda.

A proud Canadian

A proud Canadian, DeGroote retains his Canadian citizenship and passport. He has served as a director of Calgary-based Gulf Canada Resources and he has been named an Officer of the Order of Canada for his sizeable contribution to the country.

He has also received a Honourary Doctor of Law degree from McMaster University.

The Canadian connections of Michael G. DeGroote, O. C., L.L.D, also include ongoing support for Junior Achievement, $5-million funding for the Michael G. DeGroote Foundation for epilepsy research at McMaster.

There's also funding for recreation facilities at McMaster and Hillfield-Strathallan College and, of course, the Michael G. DeGroote School of Business at McMaster.

Keeping Canadian connections

DeGroote also spends at least two months every year in Canada, mainly in Burlington visiting family, including daughter Joni, son Tim, son Michael Jr. who runs housing developer Westbury International and son Gary who runs GWD Investments.

And there's no question DeGroote remains very proud and fond of Canada and Canadians.

While still a senior journalist with The Hamilton Spectator, I was fortunate to land an exclusive interview with the Canadian tycoon in Bermuda in 1990.

As Philippa – my wife and photographer – took pictures, DeGroote left no doubt that his move to Bermuda was in large part a necessity to avoid ongoing taxation in Canada, at a rate exceeding 50 per cent, which would have severely depleted his income.

He also observed that Bermuda was more conducive to estate planning and has convenient air links to Canada and all of North America.

"Canada is a hell of a great country," asserted the one-time owner of the CFL Hamilton Tiger-Cats, during an interview over lunch at Bermuda's most prestigious yacht club.

"All my early success came from there," he added.

"I'll never give up my citizenship. I'm a proud Canadian. This was not an easy decision."

Building a new business empire

DeGroote also made it clear that his relocation to Bermuda was not a retirement move.

In fact, my exclusive Spectator stories detailed a new business empire in the making that DeGroote was well on the way to establishing from the tropical pink sands of his peaceful, paradise home in Bermuda.

That new empire is being built from the foundations of his holding company Westbury (Bermuda) Limited – which controls several companies in North America and Europe – and his ownership stake in other companies, including, of course, Century Business Services Inc.

Success Story

I next caught up with DeGroote in June 1997 while working on my Success Stories book.

In fact, I again flew down to Bermuda to interview DeGroote for the book and again brought my wife - and photographer - Philippa.

To keep peace in my family, I also paid the airfare for our three children: Donovan, Sarah and Ryan, and I was fully prepared to foot the bill for their accommodations.

Enjoying life in Paradise

DeGroote had generously offered to provide accommodations for my wife and I – and then extended that offer to include our children when he later learned they were coming with us.

Without any hesitation, DeGroote put my entire family up at a scenic, luxury resort owned by Hollywood actor Michael Douglas, overlooking the pink sands of Bermuda and the deep blue water of the Atlantic Ocean.

DeGroote met our surprised looks with a grin and the comment: "It was my idea to have your family down here – I just didn't know about it."

And DeGroote also gave generously of his time, reluctantly allowing the taking of photographs (he hates having his picture taken) while our young children happily splashed in the pool at his stately manor house looking out onto Bermuda's peaceful turquoise waters.

In March 1991, within three months of moving to Bermuda, DeGroote dispelled any speculation that he'd retired: He bought control of the Republic Waste Management firm, based in Houston, Texas.

Buying Republic

"As you know, I'm a bit of a deal junkie," DeGroote confesses.

"The guy who controlled Republic was in financial trouble and wanted me to buy. I didn't really want the company so I made what I thought was a really low-ball offer – and they accepted! I was hooked again."

Within four months of the takeover, DeGroote had completely changed the board and the former president was out the door.

"I had control – but I had inherited a real dog's breakfast of a company," DeGroote recalls, shaking his head.

"It took three years to rebuild it into a viable company."

DeGroote then enlisted a brilliant former competitor, Wayne Huizenga, previously chairman of the giant Waste Management Corp., the world's largest waste management firm.

Huizenga was unwilling to invest as long as Republic's troubled hazardous waste division remained part of the company.

Companies spun out

Fortunately, DeGroote had already spun the firm out into two publicly traded entities, Republic Industries Inc. and Republic Environmental Systems Inc., the former hazardous waste division.

Content with the spinout, Huizenga invested in Republic Industries. DeGroote, who had been hands-on managing the company until then, decided at that point to turn operating management of Republic Industries over to Huizenga in May 1995.

At that time, Republic Industries' market capitalization (number of shares issued multiplied by the price per share) rang in at $110 million US. Just two years later, market capitalization had actually exceeded $10-billion US.

These incredible gains were obviously pleasing to all of the shareholders, particularly the largest single shareholder, Michael G. DeGroote, who initially held 49 per cent of the firm's shares.

A Blockbuster investment

DeGroote also profited handsomely when he invested in a little-known company Huizenga put together from a group of video stores. Both men have done very well with Blockbuster Video.

Such triumphs aside, DeGroote was still saddled with Republic Environmental, which he'd also spun out as a separate firm. Huizenga wanted nothing to do with this firm – and DeGroote wasn't too crazy about it either. What was he to do with it?

A solution arrived in the form of the Alliance group of insurers.

Merger pressure was wonderful

The privately held Alliance group wanted to go public and a merger with publicly listed Republic Environmental was seen by Alliance as the fastest way to a stock market listing.

Alliance began pressing DeGroote to make a merger happen.

For DeGroote, the pressure was wonderful. His Republic Environmental company was barely worth $12-million US on a fully capitalized basis. Shares were languishing around the $2 US mark, DeGroote recalls, "because the company had problems, real and perceived, and nobody was buying its stock."

In contrast, the Alliance group of insurance firms were enjoying annual revenue of $35.7 million US – and *they* wanted a merger. DeGroote savoured the moment, and then finally said yes.

Exceeding expectations

In an effort to kick-start the newly publicly listed International Alliance firm, DeGroote and Huizenga each invested another $5-million US "and we thought the share price might climb from $2 to perhaps as high as $6 a share," DeGroote recalls with a chuckle.

That projection would prove to be too modest.

Headlines reporting that DeGroote *and* Huizenga

were investing millions in the new firm sent share prices soaring to the $40 US mark in a few weeks.

And demand for the stock exceeded the number of shares issued.

A stock split ensued and the shares were selling in 1998 for $18 US each, or $36 US each on a pre-split basis.

"The bad news is the shares dropped to $20 from $40 – the good news is they started out at $2 and ended up at $20," notes DeGroote.

DeGroote then renamed International Alliance Services Inc. as Century Business Services (CBIZ for short) Inc., and he remains the largest single shareholder with 17 per cent of shares.

International Alliance now CBIZ

Describing the CBIZ company as "my pet," DeGroote says he plans to "spend several years building it up." He find's it's "well-managed, has great shareholder value – I'm excited about its potential."

DeGroote feels the insurance industry and business out-sourcing services are "ripe for consolidation," and he's been making that happen in a big way, shaping and redefining the industry in the process.

Diversified business

Just as DeGroote built Laidlaw into a giant by acquiring hundreds of smaller firms, CBIZ has been acquiring a steady stream of small insurance and business out-sourcing firms, integrating them into the larger company while employing economies of scale and service networks to maximize cost-efficiencies and offer customers an array of services at low cost. Indeed, CBIZ has gone well beyond the normal bounds of any insurance company by diversifying into financial planning, accounting, human resource management, payroll services and other out-sourcing services for small to mid-sized firms of five to 100 employees at very competitive, and affordable prices.

The small business community is a largely untapped market, as the normal cost of such services packages would restrict their availability to larger firms. In fact, many of the existing firms providing some or all of these services offer them exclusively to large corporations and deliberately ignore the smaller companies.

CBIZ mining untapped market

"The little guys were paying through the nose for these services, if they could get them at all," DeGroote says in an interview at his Bermuda office.

"As big providers keep raising the bar for the size of firms they'll serve, a lot more firms are left out," he adds.

"We're happy to live off these leftovers. By taking over back office paperwork, we're helping these smaller firms become competitive and grow."

From his own experience, DeGroote is well aware of how distractions, such as paperwork, can potentially sidetrack an entrepreneur from their primary role of building their business.

"We'll let these small firms concentrate on being good entrepreneurs – while we take over

All of their paperwork," asserts DeGroote, "and we're looking at a huge market for these services."

In 1997, CBIZ acquired 27 companies and added $128-million US to its revenue. Total 1997 revenue rang in at $171.1-million US, up sharply from $90.2-million US in 1996.

A year later, CBIZ acquired another 39 firms and added $255-million to revenue. Total 1998 revenue, at $359.4-million US, was more than double the revenue of the previous year.

As well, total shareholders' equity also more than doubled, to about $396-million US, up from $157.4-million US. Long-term debt remained low at just 10 per cent of total capitalization.

"Spectacular growth"

Noting that 1998 marked "the second consecutive year of spectacular growth," DeGroote was pleased with the progress being made in advancing his goal to "assemble the finest collection of professional business service firms in the United States to provide quality-outsourced services to small and mid-sized companies."

DeGroote was also pleased that "despite this rapid pace, we acquired only high-quality firms with dedicated specialists and leaders capable of implementing the next phase of our growth plan."

As pumped up as he was over 1998 results, DeGroote still added a note of caution: "While we have come a long way from the specialty insurance company we were in 1996, we still have a long way to go in providing the maximum benefit possible to each of our clients."

"This will be the focus of Century's new phase of growth – fully integrating our newly acquired companies and cross-serving our offerings to provide a full-service menu to each of our 102,00 clients," DeGroote asserts.

"By organizing our member firms and leveraging their different strengths, we are creating a company that can provide an optimal solution for most of the professional services requirements of owners and operators of small and mid-sized businesses across the United States," he explains.

Whole greater than the sum of parts

To DeGroote, the challenge ahead was to "make the whole of Century greater than the sum of its individual parts."

And in that endeavour, he has succeeded.

As impressive as nearly $360-million US revenue was in 1998, revenue shot up to a heady $546.4-million US – that's more than half-a-billion American greenbacks – in 1999.

Growth continued the next year: Revenue for the year 2000 rang in at $567.8 million US, before dipping to $526.8 million US in 2001.

CBIZ cutting debt

Revenue growth was expected to resume in 2002, despite an uncertain economy. The market growth for CBIZ services has been averaging 10 per cent growth per year, twice the rate of the GDP (gross domestic product) growth in the United States and Canada.

CBIZ is also following DeGroote's debt reduction philosophy by dramatically slashing it's overall corporate debt to just $55-million US in 2001, down from $117.5-million US in 2000.

The company continues to position itself as a fast-growing, up-and-coming industry leader in the important fields of accounting, tax, valuation, benefits administration, insurance products and consulting services.

Fuelling much of this growth is DeGroote's determination to fully integrate the companies he acquires, transforming a diverse group into a seamless whole while building on synergistic strengths, including cross-serving right across the publicly traded company.

Cross-serving taken to next level

CBIZ has already taken cross serving past the initial stage of CBIZ member firms simply referring clients to other member firms.

This approach has been advanced by CBIZ to the trusted advisor level in which "one client contact manages all of the client's outsourcing needs that we offer."

"It is only at this advance level that the client/advisor relationship can be leveraged to provide significant value to both the client and CBIZ," DeGroote explains.

Setting and achieving clear goals

He also knows the importance of continue to develop CBIZ networks in the market while also establishing the internal structure necessary to have the widespread company function as a single entity. All of these efforts can be expected to ultimately be reflected in greater value for shareholders.

"A simple but proven formula for creating long-term shareholder value in today's volatile market is setting, communicating and achieving clear performance goals," DeGroote points out. "We expect to continue to grow at a swift pace..."

Ongoing growth is based on the continuing servicing of the entrepreneur's need to focus sharply on their core business while delegating extraneous concerns to CBIZ. And this too is in keeping with DeGroote's entrepreneurial philosophy.

As DeGroote observes, there has long been a pressing need to remove obstacles such as paperwork – including such distractions as payroll, overseeing benefits plans, and dealing with accounting, tax, valuation and insurance matters – along with regulatory and government reports, or lack of education, all of which can hinder promising entrepreneurs from reaching their full potential.

"It's vital that entrepreneurs be free to focus their energy on chasing their dream," DeGroote asserts.

"We have to remove the obstacles, the distractions, and give our young entrepreneurs the tools they need to succeed."

Michael G. DeGroote's Tips for Success

1. Determine what you want to achieve. Then, clearly define your goals and foster a strong desire to succeed. Focus on priorities.

2. Start or acquire a business that suits your interests and abilities, one, which you will genuinely enjoy investing a great deal of your time into making it a success.

3. Devote the time needed to create, develop and grow your business venture.

4. Apply determination, a methodology to achieve what you set out to do, and a consistency of approach to carry out your goals and objectives.

5. Expect to work long and hard achieve these goals and sacrifice much of your "personal" time.

6. Make sure you link up with the right people whose skill sets complement your own.

7. Be certain everyone involved has a clear understanding of the company's direction and your own expectations.

8. Realize your employees generate profit. You and your management are overhead.

9. Keep managers and layers of management to a minimum to improve communications.

10. Do the most with the least. Corporate office people should perform real tasks and jobs.

11. Focus on creating shareholder value.

12. Do not over extend yourself. Too many entrepreneurs take on too much debt far too early and find they cannot handle the carrying costs. Avoid unnecessary or premature expenditures.

13. Keep your overhead low, your operations lean and mean.

14. Make commitments and keep them. Be as good as your word.

15. Grow your business gradually without resorting to excessive financing.

16. Focus on creating high quality services and products. Meet customer needs and desires.

17. Whenever embarking on new acquisitions or a change of direction, do your homework. This includes the normal due diligence process along with market research.

18. Integrate your acquisitions into the master company and centralize as you grow.

19. Be willing to take on risk. But try to ensure it's manageable risk that's needed to take advantage of business opportunities.

20. Foster teamwork and put in place the best team you can assemble.

21. Listen carefully to employees, assist them where possible and reward them for achievements.

22. Never lock yourself in to anything. Be prepared to change.

23. Do not brood over mistakes. Focus on solutions. Make work life enjoyable and satisfying.

24. Take a hard look in the mirror and raise your own expectations of yourself. Says DeGroote: "When you're through improving, you're through."

Manor House Publishing
(905) 648-2193

www.ingramcontent.com/pod-product-compliance
Lightning Source LLC
Chambersburg PA
CBHW031244290426
44109CB00012B/425